WEST GRINSTEAD LOCAL HISTORY GROUP

WHEN THE WHISTLE BLEW

The story of Dial Post, Littleworth, Partridge Green & West Grinstead in World War 2.

West Grinstead Local History Group,
C/o Parish Office, Village Hall,
High Street, Partridge Green,
West Sussex, RH13 8HX

E-mail: wglhg1@tesco.net

First published in Great Britain in 2008 by West Grinstead
Local History Group.

978-0-9561142-0-4

CONTENTS

SECTION	CHAPTER	PAGE
	Foreword	2
	Introduction	3
	Timeline and Currency	5
1 — PEOPLE	Children	7
	Women's Organisations	20
	Farming	23
	Wartime Memories of Needs Farm	37
	Trade and Commerce	50
	Doctors and Nurses	57
	The Parish Church during the War	62
	War Memorials	68
	Partridge Green Methodist Chapel	80
	Local Travel during the War	82
	Policing	88
	Home Guard	91
	The Auxiliary Fire Service	101
	Dial Post during World War 2	103
	The Military Presence in this Area	110
	Parish Council	117
	Helping the War Effort	119
2 — EVENTS	What Happened Where	123
	The Junkers 88 Crash	133
	Operation Sidecar	138
APPENDIX 1	Partridge Green Wartime Telephone Nos.	149
APPENDIX 2	Acknowledgments	154
APPENDIX 3	Authors	155

Foreword

In 2005 there was a concerted effort, funded in part by the Heritage Lottery Fund, but only made practical by a substantial amount of volunteer effort, to capture memories of Britain during World War 2. The armed services had seen a similar groundswell of recording and capturing in 1999, on the realisation that those who served would soon no longer be around, or be able to retain their memories. By 2005 there was a general awareness that the story of the Home Front was largely ignored in the national consciousness.

West Grinstead Local History Group didn't exist in 2005, but its formation in 2006 and the desire to do something more than just hold talks led to a World War 2 weekend in the summer of that year, with the decision to research and write this book following soon afterwards.

The book that follows not only opens up a new vista on West Grinstead Parish history but also reveals a half forgotten landscape. After reading this book you will no longer be able to look at the buildings, homes or countryside in the same way again, for over there a bomb fell, there the Canadians were stationed, right there the Home Guard patrolled and in the distance the German plane crashed. It should also be remembered that West Grinstead was a border parish, as it lay on the boundary of the military zone; any further south and you needed a pass to enter.

There are here not just memories of adult players in the drama, but also some of children who lived in an era when children were seen but not heard, and who now have the opportunity to have their say. It is through the rich texture of the voices; those who for decades have been silent except to their families; that the real depth to this book is provided.

It would be invidious to identify any one account more than any other as every one adds to creating a picture of war torn West Grinstead Parish. The phrase "war torn" might seem glib, or arguably better used in areas that saw massive destruction, but it is the right phrase to use here, for West Grinstead was war torn – the war did tear the social, economic and psychological fabric that had created pre war West Grinstead – that very damage allowing the parish (and the country) to be made anew. Imagine just for a moment knowing that at any hour a bomb could fall out of the sky – the constant threat of danger where your home wasn't your sanctuary, where friends and neighbours went off to fight and may never come back, where your village was swamped with foreigners who spoke differently, dressed differently and being exotic created a certain frisson within the population. This book allows just a glimpse of that, for that is all it can do, but what a glimpse it gives through the half closed eyes caused by time and age.

Providing a backdrop to these half remembered accounts is a wealth of official reports, statistics and government advice and practice. Often lying dormant in archives these sources have been successfully quarried by members of the group providing us with the all important understanding of why things were done. Alongside these reports on agriculture, civil defence etc. are the accounts from the parish magazine and local press which have also been mined for supplementary information. The book is a group effort and this clearly comes across as you read these authored chapters.

History is not the past, the past is the past, and simple listing of events is a chronology — history is the evaluation of events to create a public narrative which helps us to understand, explain and explore the past. The West Grinstead Local History Group has with this book made an indelible mark on the history of the parish – no-one working on this period in this area can ignore this book, just as we cannot, nor should we ignore the contribution made by those who served on the Home Front.

Jeremy Knight
Curator, Horsham Museum

Introduction

When the West Grinstead Local History Group was formed in 2006 it was decided that the first project would be a study of the Parish during World War 2. It was considered that the experiences of those who lived locally during the conflict should be gathered as less and less would remain in the future.

Of course there have been many books written on the conflict and by most standards West Grinstead was a minor backwater during that terrible time. However, whilst it did not suffer the devastation of many large towns, the War did cause social disruption and the area probably changed more than during any other similar period of its history.

Even before the start of the War there was the invasion of evacuees from London and the clash of cultures was dramatic and initially seemed intolerable to locals and evacuees alike. Of course in time the "townies" integrated to the point that most found the rural life enjoyable and they were accepted. There followed a second military invasion, mainly by Canadian soldiers, that again was difficult for both sides. In the end both sets of "invaders" settled most of their differences with the local people. Indeed a number of evacuees stayed in the area after the War and several local girls married Canadian soldiers. Interestingly the P.O.W.s employed locally appear to have fitted in quite well.

The Parish in 1939 was essentially an agricultural area and the wartime needs caused dramatic changes to agriculture. Sheep largely disappeared early in the War as the government demanded the growth of crops to reduce the need for imports. At the same time, with a large part of the agricultural labour force joining the forces, farm mechanisation increased rapidly. When peace came most of these changes were not reversed and many fewer of the local population were employed in agriculture.

In writing this book Group members have interviewed locals who lived through the War. We have also been able to make use of a number of short essays that had been published in the West Grinstead Newsletter, transcriptions of talks and other published and unpublished memories. The contributors were often reflecting on events that took place over 60 years ago and the details cannot always be verified, so there may be some grey areas but we considered it best to change the content as little as possible. It was considered important to keep to contributors' words as far as possible. The authors of each section have been given free rein to use the style that they are happy with. It is hoped therefore that the various formats make the book more interesting and are not looked at with a jaundiced eye.

Thanks are due to all of the contributors and particularly the Group members who laboured so long on their researches, then glued their findings together. A few details have been given of most of the major players at the end of the book.

We would like to give a special thanks to Jeremy Knight from Horsham Museum for his help in forming the Group and guiding us through the minefield of producing a book. Christine Knight, the head of Jolesfield School allowed us access to old school records from the period of the evacuees. We also enjoyed cooperation from the School with joint activities for the World War 2 exhibition that we staged.

Cliff White author of "When the Siren Sounded" also gave us invaluable help especially with regard to "Operation Sidecar", the glider landings around Dial Post.

We had been contacted by a local lady who remembered seeing the gliders landing but could find no information of the event. We also had little success until Cliff gave us details of an aerial photo in the Knepp Castle archives. Eventually we were able to get detailed information on this large D-Day rehearsal that few local people knew about. This led us to Knepp Castle where Sir Charles Burrell gave us very helpful access to the archives.

Finally, you may be wondering why we called the book "When the Whistle Blew". Below are some memories from Claire Walton that explain the title and also give a start from the first day of the War. I would add that several people had particular memories of the "whistle blowing!"

Some Memories of World War 2 In and Around the Parish of West Grinstead

By Claire Walton (from the Parish Newsletter – Summer 1996)

When War was declared on Sunday 3rd Sept 1939 I felt the impossible had come to pass. My sister had left home some time earlier and was waiting to start her nursing training in London. I was about to start my last year as a pupil at Horsham High School. We had been brought up on tales of the horrors of WWI, but may have felt a bit awed by all the memories recounted, never believing we would find ourselves in a similar situation one day, sooner rather than later.

My mother and aunt listened avidly to Neville Chamberlain's historic broadcast, obviously distressed at all his words could mean. I remember I was having a bath and definitely did not take in the implications of what he said. That morning the wind must have been in the north, for very shortly afterward we heard the Horsham air raid siren sounding its first alert of the War. I have never got out of the bath so quickly and any doubting illusions I may have harboured for a few minutes were gone for good. Thankfully, after a short time we heard the "All Clear", but I think my age group knew from then on that our situation was Serious Business and this was For Real.

In West Grinstead we only heard the siren if the wind was in the right direction or we were out of doors. We had an Air Raid Warden, Ernest Barnard. He was chauffeur to Capt George Hornung who had lived at Glebe House. Mr. Barnard and his family lived in one of the cottages at the Glebe – I cannot remember which one. Anyway, as soon as an Alert was phoned through to him he would cycle from the Glebe, along Steyning Road to Park Lane, all around the station and kennels and on to Westlands and Clock House, unless he had time to go further. He blew a police whistle and frantically waved a football-type rattle; if he saw anyone outside he would shout "Take cover". It all sounds a very amateur and even comic effort, but I am sure it was the best that could be done in a very scattered rural patch. Needless to say, Mr. B was exhausted by his efforts to warn as many as possible and I have no recollection of ever hearing an "All Clear" from him!

We would like to give a special acknowledgment to David Meed from Dial Post for kindly designing the cover.

World War 2 Timeline

The information below is a general guide to some of the main events that affected the local population.

1939

July	Women's Land Army formed
2nd September	Evacuation of children and their families to this area began.
3rd September	War declared.
1st October	Conscription starts.
18th December	Canadian troops start to arrive in England.

1940

8th January	Start of food rationing. The items rationed and allowances for each category varied considerably from time to time. In fact food rationing was not finally dispensed with until 9 years after the end of World War 2.
11th May	Neville Chamberlain resigns and Winston Churchill becomes Prime Minister.
20th May	Local Defence Volunteers (LDV) formed. The name was later changed to the Home Guard.
26th May - 3rd June	Dunkirk evacuation of the British Expeditionary Force and French Army remnants.
1st June	Signposts and place name signs removed or obliterated.
10th July - 31st October	Official British dates for the Battle of Britain. In fact the large scale bombing of British cities continued until late March 1942, and this is considered by Germany to be the end of the Battle. Bombing continued but on a much smaller scale, often as "hit and run" attacks.
26th September	St. Hugh's Charterhouse Monastery bombed.

1941

29th May	St Hugh's Charterhouse Monastery bombed again.
1st June	Start of clothes rationing.
22nd June	Germany declares war on Russia.
28th July	Junkers 88 crashes near corner of Lock Lane and Bines Road.
3rd December	Compulsory War Service for women.

1943

6th June	The German occupation of mainland Europe prevented the import of wines from most traditional suppliers. The success of the army in North Africa allowed the first "fruits of war" – wine imports from Algeria.

1944

January – July	As forces were built up for the invasion of Europe, the area adjacent to the South Coast of England became a restricted area. Entry was prohibited to non-residents without special permission. At this time everyone had Identity Cards with their addresses. West Grinstead was just outside of this restricted zone, but anywhere further south (e.g. Henfield) was included.
6th June	D Day.
June - March 1945	V1 flying bomb attacks on England.
6th July	V1 explodes in field adjacent to Church Road.
September - March 1945	V2 rocket attacks on England.
3rd December	Home Guard "stood down".

1945

8th May	VE Day (Victory in Europe).
15th August	VJ Day (Victory over Japan).

World War 2 Currency

The units of currency were the farthing (¼d), penny (d), the shilling (s) and the pound (£).

4 farthings = 1d

12d = 1s

20s = £1

"Copper" coins: Farthing (¼d), ha'penny (½d), penny, threepenny piece.

"Silver" coins: Sixpenny piece, shilling, florin (2s), half crown (2s 6d).

Notes: 10 shillings (10s), 1 pound (£1), 5 pounds (£5).

During the 1930s silver coins had been replaced by identical looking cupro-nickel versions. The exception was the small 3d coin ("3d Joey"). In 1941 this was phased out and replaced by a larger, but less expensive to make, copper coin.

Silver (left) and copper 3d coins.

6

Children

By Barbara Berry

Whilst Britain may have been slow in arming to meet the threat of war there were many advanced preparations on the civilian front. As the leaflet "Transfer of Population in time of War" on the next page shows, arrangements had begun in 1938 for evacuation, so that this could be published in January 1939. By April the parish magazine reported that the Local Education Authority had asked that the local church schools be used as centres for evacuation in case of emergency.

Indeed the war started a week early in Partridge Green with the invasion of pupils and teachers from the Brixton School in London. The children arrived with labels around their necks, accompanied by their teachers. There were also a number of complete families – usually less the father. It was left to the WVS (Women's Voluntary Service) to take the children round the village and find people with a spare bedroom to take the children, trying if possible to keep siblings together. Several had to be re-homed, as they were incompatible with the first family to whom they were given. The children at first treated the evacuation as an adventure and could not understand why their mothers were crying when they saw them off. Talking now about the events of those days in 1939 recalls painful memories that have been deeply hidden for 60 years, exposing the trauma of separation and isolation. Some were very homesick and hated country life – they soon returned home; some parents demanded their children be returned to them. I am sure the majority eventually settled quite happily, although others never got used to the quietness of the countryside, the lack of traffic and (sometimes) of street lights or the distance from the shops, etc.

At that time there were two state schools in the parish – Jolesfield, Partridge Green and Swallows Lane, Dial Post. Their arrival brought chaos to the Jolesfield Church of England School as it received the bulk of the school age evacuees. It was not equipped to double in size overnight, so several schemes were tried but the best one seemed to be that of using the village hall, the Methodist hall and Jolesfield School for classrooms. The Jolesfield children used the school one week whilst the Brixton children used the halls, changing over on alternate weeks.

The following letter was published in the parish magazine when the newcomers were settled;

"The Green Man",
Partridge Green.
18/9/1939.

Dear Bishop Wood,

I should like to express on behalf of myself, my staff and the children, through the medium of the Parish Magazine, our very sincere gratitude to the people of Partridge Green for their unstinted help and many kindnesses to us in our plight as evacuees.

We know that in many cases great sacrifices have had to be made to accommodate us, but they have been made with a cheerfulness that speaks eloquently of the total practical Christianity of all concerned.

May God bless you all for your goodness. Yours sincerely,
*   H. Greenwood,*
Headmaster of Brixton Parish Church School.

This leaflet published by the Ministry of Health in January, 1939 shows that at least in planning for evacuation the Government was well prepared.

OUTLINE OF GOVERNMENT SCHEME

3

The arrangements which are being made provide for dispersal from the crowded towns where the results of air attack would be most serious. In this movement priority will be given to children, and school children will, as far as possible, be moved school by school, accompanied by their teachers and other helpers. Where this arrangement is made householders will be asked to board and lodge the children. Homes are to be found for them in the districts to which they are to be taken: that is why arrangements must be planned in advance. Householders who provide such homes will be paid by the Government at the rate of 10s. 6d. a week where one child is taken and 8s. 6d. a week for each child where more than one child is taken.

Children under school age will be accompanied by their mothers or some other person who will be responsible for looking after them. In these cases the householder will only be asked to provide lodging, not board, and payment will be made at the rate of 5s. a week for each adult and 3s. a week for each child. Payment at the rate of 5s. a week will be made by the Government where the householder provides lodging for a teacher or helper accompanying a party of school children.

Arrangements for the necessary transport and for increased supplies of food to be made available for shopkeepers will be made by the Government.

Form Ev. 1.
51—2128

We must prepare in good time against the possibility of war, however remote that possibility may be. Most people will necessarily be kept where they are by their duties, but there will be many in the big cities who, both in the national interest and on grounds of humanity, should go to places where they will be rather safer from air attack.

Children must come first. That, I am sure, will be agreed by all, and I feel sure too that we can rely on willing help from all. Though we shall use empty houses and camps as far as we can, we must look in the main to householders to receive these children. We will do all we can to lessen the inconvenience and spread the burden evenly. That is one of the main reasons why we must plan in advance.

The attached notes explain in a general way the arrangements which the Government has in mind. They will not of course come into operation unless and until an emergency arises. If an emergency does come, an announcement will be made that the arrangements which have been planned are to be put into operation. In every case as much notice as possible will be given to householders.

Walter Elliot

MINISTRY OF HEALTH.
January, 1939.

The journey to school for children living in the outskirts of the village was by Mr. Burdfield's canvas canopied lorry with slatted benches to sit on and exhaust fumes pouring over the tail board making them very pleased to arrive.

All the children had gas masks, the younger ones having the "Mickey Mouse" type. They had to carry them with them all the time. Messrs. Darrington and Kidd, the A.R.P. (Air Raid Protection) wardens, challenged anyone caught without their mask. On January 26th 1941 the children had a shelter practice and the A.R.P. warden examined all the children's gas masks. In the School Punishment Book one boy was given one stroke on each hand with the cane for forgetting his gas mask! This may seem harsh but other entries in the book indicate that there was a very different attitude to discipline at that time. Two boys were given two strokes on each hand for stealing one apple each from a tree on their way to school. Another two boys received one stroke on each hand for playing in the rain and getting soaking wet. In 1942 eight children were caned for leaving school to go scrumping for pears at Medway House. Others in 1943 were caned for repeatedly stealing eggs from "Greenfinch's Hut". Things were much stricter in those days!

It was some time before a shelter was built for the school but by August, 1940 trenches had been dug by volunteers adjacent to the two schools for sheltering in during air raids. People were very proud of them and they became "sites worth seeing". Later proper brick shelters were provided.

Cooking lessons for the girls were cancelled as the Government requisitioned the parish room and the boys' woodwork lessons at Steyning were also cancelled because of petrol rationing and the requisition of the woodwork room. Cooking and woodwork were later restarted, the boys cycling to Steyning under the supervision of a teacher.

The evacuees and the Partridge Green children did not get on together very well. The Brixton children were used to living in the city and found the countryside very quiet and boring. It was the first time that many of the evacuees realized that milk came from cows! The local children found the Brixton children difficult to understand with their cockney accents and their ability and willingness to fight. One method of fighting was with their blue mackintoshes, which they rolled into a ball and tied up with their belts, which had buckles, and in the words of one Partridge Green lad; "we clouted them with them and the buckles hurt." Very few early friendships between the local children and the evacuees were formed but in time both sides learnt to live together and accept that they spoke differently and had different interests. However, the London children may not have been as lacking in culture as the locals initially thought. They demonstrated their skills on various occasions. For example, on July 17th 1940 the Brixton School Drill and Dance Display Team gave a display at Jolesfield House and on January 15th 1941 they did a Nativity Play in the Village Hall. On June 12th a P.T. and Dancing display was given at Jolesfield House.

Evacuee Sheila Oldfield with Jess Merritt in his Home Guard Uniform

Surprisingly, although the children did not get on with the evacuees they seemed to have a good relationship with the Prisoners of War. One in particular, who worked on the Lock Estate, spoke very good English and became good friends with several children. The P.O.W.s came from the camp in Billingshurst and were brought and collected by lorry. They used to speak to the children as they were coming home from school and whilst they were waiting to be picked up by the lorry to return to the camp. They met by the railway line. In their brown uniforms with a yellow circle on the back they were easily recognisable. In their spare time they made toys for the children and did odd jobs for the villagers.

Continued on p.11

Extracts from an interview with Roy Coultrup.

Roy lived in Church Road, Partridge Green.

The situation was so bad that Roy was recruited to the Home Guard at a very early age. The pompoms on his footwear suggest that he may have been loaned to the Greek Army.

My dad was in the Home Guard, this was early on when the bomber crashed and he went there, all hero like, and picked up a boot, but there was a foot still in it, so that was the end of that for him, my dad lost interest in the proceedings for a bit. The German had a little envelope with a heart on it that was obviously a keepsake, it is only a little bronze thing with a little heart on it, dad found it when he had recovered himself from the foot in the boot episode.

The plane crashed on the cottages over the forge – now gone. We used to enjoy watching the blacksmith at work. The cottages across the road are laid back a bit and the bomber crashed there. The engine went through one of the bungalows of a friend. There was a picture in the paper of his mum in bed with his brother and sister, with the engine of this plane over in the corner.

We loved picking up bits of shell case and the 'windows'. I picked up a complete packet in the corner of the cricket field near the pond. We usually found loads of bits but this one dropped out of the plane and they hadn't pulled the elastic bands or whatever it was that kept it together and it landed as a pack covered in brown waterproof paper. Finding that as a kid was quite an adventure and it ended up on the Christmas tree. To find a complete pack was wonderful. We also loved the bits of Perspex which we burnt holes in the middle of to make rings.

We had one POW as a friend, he worked down Lock Estate and we used to meet him up on the railway bridge. I remember he had this brown uniform with a big yellow circle on the back. He spoke English very well. As far as we were concerned he wasn't a Nazi, he was just a nice chap.

The Canadians used to come to do their training and they had their faces blacked out with cork, which we found out later, so of course all us kids were looking for a bit of cork so we could burn it so we could all walk round with black faces too. The only toys that we had were made for us by the Canadian soldiers up at Knepp Castle. One made me a smashing tommy gun, which I regret never keeping. It was really good, it had a wooden bit and as you fired it you would turn the handle and it sort of crcrcrcred. It was a really good effort and I had it all during the war.

The Yanks used to chuck us chewing gum. I had never seen chewing gum before and we went to school chewing gum and a chap called George Gumbrell was there, the headmaster, and he was not pleased to see us all sitting there doing this. He confiscated the chewing gum whereupon all the mums went to the school and demanded that he gave it back as it wasn't his to take away, so we got it back again. We had never seen chewing gum and all these Yanks went through in their jeeps and what not, probably this was for D-Day, and would chuck it out in great big packets. You didn't just get a little bit you got a great big packet. They were very good, the stuff they used to give out. They stopped as they went through the village and the mums made them cups of tea and they were so generous.

Some evacuees did of course get on with the families they were boarded with and stayed on after the war. Marie Pearson lived with Mr. & Mrs. T. Child in South Street and later in Blanches Road. Joan Cavalier was with Mrs. C. Hemsley in Weald Cottage, Bines Road and was there when the Junkers engine came through the bedroom window. Rosemary Sayers who lives in The Rise grew up with Joan almost like an older sister. Lily Baldwin was at first in the cottages opposite Tidey's Mill and later with the Kierneys in a house on the north side of the lane running off Church Road down to the old railway line. She stayed on after the war and worked in a shop in Horsham. Mrs. Gale came with her two daughters, Jean and Gloria, and lived in Oxford House in the High Street. Gloria married Archie Andrews and lived in The Rise, but unfortunately she died some years ago. Jean married John Fisher and they still live in Littleworth Lane. Mrs. Powell came with two children, Fred and Beryl and they settled in Blanches Road.

There were two Hoskins families. Bert with his wife and son Philip, and Bert was a porter at Partridge Green for many years and lived in Railway Cottages. Bert's brother and his family lived first in the old Pullman carriages on Moat Farm and then in Blanches Road. Their son Bill married and went to live in Henfield. Mrs. Pullen and her daughter Dorothy lived in the house east of the chapel and her two elder daughters Heather and Sheila lived with Mr. & Mrs. Tidey in Southview Cottage, and later moved across the road to Mr. & Mrs. Burdfield in Gresham House.

The boys and girls had separate playgrounds, the girls having the better one, with a four foot high wall separating them. Children used to take a potato with their name on into school in the morning and two senior boys who looked after the old boiler in the "stoke hole" would cook them and hand them out at playtime, some half-cooked and some burnt black, but no-one seemed to mind.

On the whole the children seemed to think the war was very exciting and when planes crashed they used to hunt for souvenirs. Pieces of Perspex were valuable finds and they could be moulded into toys. Bits of broken planes made good toys for the boys who used to "swap" their finds. All the children were urged to look out for "spies" and report on any strangers they saw in the village.

During the Battle of Britain the children used to watch the dog fights played overhead and collected many bits and pieces. Planes used to drop packets of aluminium foil ("windows" used to confuse radar) whose contents used to be widely spread over the fields, but one boy managed to find a complete package and was, as a result, very popular at the time. The package was eventually given pride of place on their Christmas tree.

Living in the country, the children never went hungry, as most people grew their own vegetables. Rabbits and chickens supplemented their meat ration. Those whose parents worked on the farms used to get extra milk and eggs. Families used to swap foods of which they had a surplus for things that they found hard to come by.

The Canadian soldiers based at Knepp Castle developed a good relationship with the children although their occasional rowdy behaviour did frighten some of the younger ones. They used to collect the children at Christmas time, give them a party and sing carols with them. Many children had lovely toys made for them by the soldiers. There is little doubt that the Canadians hoped that their friendship with the children would warm their relationship with the whole local population. Thus, on July 2nd 1942 Major Jones, attached to the 1st Canadian Division, gave a talk at the school as part of their attempt at better P.R. with the locals. Of course it also helped to soften the homesickness of soldiers far away from families for long periods. The Americans used to practise in the village in camouflage, rehearsing for D-Day, and the boys copied them by using burnt corks with which to black their faces.

Chocolate was in plentiful supply to the American and Canadian troops and they generously gave much of it to the children. When the Canadian and American troops were walking through the village they used to be given cups of tea by mothers who were often rewarded with cigarettes.

The Canadians were less popular as it was said that they used to get drunk and make a lot of noise on their way back to Knepp Castle but that did not worry the children. The Americans often gave the children things and they learnt not to tell their mothers in case they confiscated them.

In Dial Post an emergency supply of "Big Army Biscuits" in a sealed tin was kept on the top shelf of the shop. When it became "out of date" it was opened and given to the school to sell to the children at break times for a ha'penny each and they were very much enjoyed.

On January 23rd 1941 a school garden was started with borrowed tools at Jolesfield. In April the same year 10 rods (about 252 sq.m.) of new land was purchased for the school garden and the children worked in the garden both during term time and also in the holidays. Visits of the School Attendance Officer were less frequent due to petrol rationing. The children had to cycle to Henfield accompanied by a teacher to play football and cricket matches.

Football matches were also played between Jolesfield School and Brixton School. The two schools were eventually merged on 29th March 1943 and 34 evacuees and 1 teacher came onto the Jolesfield books, making a total of 180 pupils. The school then occupied Jolesfield School and the Village Hall. Jolesfield School was granted one extra teacher.

On July 5th 1944 a "Doodle Bug" damaged Miss Rhodes' bungalow in Church Road and slightly damaged Jolesfield School. Fortunately it happened early in the morning before the children were at school. (See "Events" section.)

Children going on to further education, mainly those wishing to go on to University, had to travel to Horsham or Steyning. The train service and the bus service from Partridge Green to Horsham continued during the war, with the odd interruption. The bus service managed to continue despite the black out making it difficult for passengers to know exactly where they were after dark.

Claire Walton remembers that air raid shelters were always used for school examinations and during air raids for lessons for the whole school. When air raids were expected the children had to go to the shelters with their gas masks on. This was quite difficult for those who wore glasses as they had to take their glasses off before putting their masks on and this made them always the last children to arrive in the shelter. The situation was at its worst of course during the Battle of Britain in 1940 – 41.

We have included several people's childhood recollections of the war. Although this gives some duplication it was felt that these memories give the best record of childhood at that time.

An Evacuee's View

Extract from an interview with Sid and Jeanne Savage who still live locally

Sid Savage photographed in 1948

Sid Savage: I was evacuated to Copyhold, Lock Lane with Mrs. Langton. We came down from London on the Saturday and the war broke out on the Sunday. The whole family, all of them except my Dad. As far as I know we all just came and we unloaded at the village hall and then I suppose they took them to their individual places from the village hall, but we were one of the last being a family of four children and Mum. To be kept together was quite an achievement, and to find someone to take you in.

We used to go to the school three days one week and then the village hall two days and then the next week Brixton would have the school for three days and they would come down to the village hall for two days. The schooling was all done between the school and the village hall really, shared between the two schools.

Later we moved to the cottage next to the Windmill pub in Littleworth. The searchlight was behind there and the Windmill. The only gun they had there was a Lewis gun, and then later on a Vickers gun, I don't think they dumped it until later on, but they were instructed not to fire it at any aircraft unless they were attacked, but they did open fire on one when the children were out on the playing fields at Jolesfield. We were all out in that playing field, playing at dinnertime and these two German aircraft came over. That is when they fired on West Grinstead station and killed the train driver.

The Canadians were at Shermanbury Grange, but to see a lot you had to be on the A281 — that's where all the tanks went.

Jeanne Savage: We used to get them round here because we had a ditch outside and if they were told they could have a rest they used to sit by the side of the ditch and then Mum and Auntie Jess next door used to run out with jugs of lemonade for them and us kids used to cadge sweets from them.

My Dad used to bring some soldiers home here for meals in the evening. You never knew who he would bring home for meals. Then they were all up at Knepp Castle. They used to put on a Christmas Party for all the children of the estate workers, and by then Dad was works manager at the Castle so we used to go up there. They used to give us a bag with an orange, which we had not seen for years, and give us pencils, crayon books and a bit of fruit.

Jeanne Hemsley (later Savage) and evacuee Pam Burrows on the right.

Dial Post School 1943

Back row: *Mrs Creasey, John Thornton, Nelson Riddle, Sheila Stone, ? Dearing, Christine Band, Pat Sturt, Ena Neale, May Longhurst, Margaret Wood, Ruth Field, Merrick Warnett, Ray Edmonds, Mrs Treadwell*

Centre Row: *? Terry, Joan Puttock, Gwen Puttock, Rosina Demonds, Len Neale, ? Dearing, ? Terry, ? Dearing, Lilian Reagraves, ? Dearing, Silvia Band*

Front Row: *Jean Penny, John Penny, Norah Wayman, Robert Thornton, Kathy Burrows, David Barnsley, Norman Birkett, Bruce Di-Rose, Ronnie Fisher*

Partridge Green Invaded

By Beryl Bazen (née Powell)

When Hitler got serious about bombing the London docks my father decided it was time to move his young family (myself 3 years, my brother 8 years and mum) to safer ground. "We'll go to Partridge Green" he said, "Hitler will never find it – it's not even on the map!"

My father, who termed himself a 'Pioneer of the Electrical Age', had visited Partridge Green whilst cable-laying, to bring the first supply of electricity, around the UK.

Public transport was out of the question, London Bridge station was overwhelmed, so father found one of his contractors who was able to take us part of the way (Redhill) in an open lorry. This was my first recollection, probably picking up vibes from a very emotionally charged atmosphere. My baby cousin Derek was being carried, as his big sister was in his pram having just had her appendix out. The hospital had been bombed, so her stitches were taken out by the family doctor working under a bed-sheet canopy held over the patient by my aunt and uncle to stop pieces of plaster falling onto the wound.

I have no recollection of the ongoing train journey but I seem to recall being in the village hall sleeping on the floor with many other families. My mother was ever in admiration for Mrs Langton and her mother of Copyhold, Lock Lane, who walked the floor all night, comforting and filling needs. I believe a Mrs Darrington was the area billeting officer. Her role was to tell unsuspecting householders that they had room to take in a given number of strangers whether they wanted to or not. We and five other families were placed in a condemned thatched cottage two doors from the Windmill public house in Littleworth.

The men folk having returned to work in the capital, the city mothers enquired about the shops. A bicycle was produced to carry their errands from Partridge Green, which at the time consisted of the High Street and South Street. Primus stoves, oil lamps, bucket toilets and bicycles were unknown quantities. My aunt, the only cyclist, set off to a chorus of cheers.

The Retreat

It seems all but a few of the invaders from London returned or moved on and the rest of us settled down into village life. We moved to Mrs Dory's house, 1 Maple Cottages in the High Street by the post office. My father brought electricity into the house, and joy of joys down the garden was a flush toilet. The vicar called, possibly urged on by lisle-stockinged, less glamorous mums, to question my mother's morals! Here she was, young and attractive, wearing lipstick and possibly worse, smoking. She must have won him over as Rev. Lewis became a regular visitor to sit and have a cuppa.

Next door to us lived the amazing Ducky Burdfield. The village was dominated by Sayers and Burdfields, mostly related. We had bread delivered by Lou Burdfield, our milk by Nim. Jack sang bass in the church choir and Ducky did everything else! He was the builder, undertaker, school transport (a lorry), church organist and choir master. My brother and I sang in the church choir whilst my mother kept chickens and cooked for the British Restaurant in Horsham. We were accepted.

My lovely grandmother was also with us and was fondly known by the whole village as 'Gran Green' as she always had a few pence or a sweet to give away to the children. Family and friends descended at every opportunity to get a good night's sleep away from the blitz and my aunt (the late Rose Brown) was billeted with us whilst stationed as a WAAF at Faygate Air Force Base. Goodness knows where we all slept!

Dad was away for long periods (travel was not encouraged or so easy then), but when home for weekends he ran Saturday night dances in the village hall. At Christmas there was a huge party open to all, also in the village hall, and everyone who could get away attended, including Canadian soldiers stationed at the Grange. These young men away from family and friends made wooden toys and threw a lovely party for all us Jolesfield school children.

Post war, having no London home and my father working wherever a new power station required his engineering skills, my parents decided to settle in Partridge Green and bought Huffs Wood. My father and uncle envisaged two bungalows, but the powers that be envisaged an egg-packing station. By this time I was 11 and my brother 16 and we were still in two rooms at Mrs Dory's house.

To compensate a little for the compulsory purchase order which put a stop to our dream home we were allocated a newly built council owned house in Blanches Close to rent. Now, 1948 and we had a bathroom and two flush toilets!

My father, the complete towny, loved the countryside but sadly died early; my mother stayed in the village and died aged 85 in 1993 whilst happily residing in Peacocks sheltered housing complex.

Some Memories of Growing Up in the War-Torn Years

By Doug Pennifold

War was declared at 11am on Sunday September 3rd 1939. For years I was convinced I was in St Michael's and the vicar made the announcement; I am now not too sure because in my mind it all bears a striking similarity to the scene in the film 'Mrs Miniver'. The effects of coming war were apparent in Partridge Green a week earlier with the arrival of the evacuees from Brixton. As children it was all different and exciting and the fact I had to move into a single bed in my parents' room while my brothers shared a room to allow two strangers to have the third bedroom did not bother me at all. Londoners were strange to us; they understood so little about the country and had so much to tell us about city life. What also remains vivid in my mind is that most of them (certainly our two) had about one month's pocket money which meant for a short while they were all stocked up with sweets and chocolate bars so it paid to be their friends.

Their arrival naturally brought chaos to Jolesfield C of E School which was not equipped for a sudden doubling of its intake. Initially a scheme was devised where we, the locals, used the school in the mornings under our headmaster Mr Garton and the evacuees used it in the afternoon under their headmaster Mr Greenwood. The following week the timing was reversed. I remember how difficult it was to return home from a morning's play in time to get to school for the afternoon. After a time the village hall and the Methodist chapel hall were brought into use and I recall we would have one week at the school and the following week in the halls.

An early wartime action was the need for air raid protection and the fathers set to work to dig a shelter on the land immediately to the south of the school with the entrance opposite one of the doors from a cloakroom. I remember having a practice visit into the shelter but come the winter rains my recollection is that it was knee deep in water. I wonder how many projects like that were worked on in haste with huge enthusiasm but were not well thought out.

We were all fitted out with gas masks and were instructed on wearing them. I always felt I would suffocate in one and am thankful that we never had to wear them. Small children were given Mickey Mouse style masks; they may have looked alright but must have been terrifying to wear. Gas masks had to be carried at all times and we would be challenged by Messrs Darrington and Kidd, the ARP wardens, if we were caught without them.

During the first year of the war we put up with quite a lot of inconveniences (hardships by modern standards) but the realities of the real war had not hit us. Our problems were coping with evacuees, shortages and rationing. Not that the latter hit us as hard as it did the town and city dwellers. We kept chickens (for which we got a chicken feed ration), often managed to get wild rabbits and kept a large number of tame rabbits for the table. Everybody grew as much food as they could and many households were self sufficient in vegetables. Nothing was wasted – apples, pears and plums were bottled and I recall picking quite enormous quantities of blackberries. Because of the shortage of Kilner jars good use was made of candle wax to seal the jars.

Everything and everybody was working in the name of 'The War Effort'. We had our own LDV (Local Defence Volunteers), the forerunner of the Home Guard but there were no uniforms, only armbands. The equipment consisted of a sentry box positioned on the top of the station bridge, a rifle with a bayonet but no ammunition and a great deal of enthusiasm (everybody had to belong to something). The Partridge Green Auxiliary Fire Service was formed based in the garage attached to the Station Hotel (now the Partridge) and Herbert Mitchell the butcher was an inspector in the special constabulary.

My brothers joined the Air Force cadets at Henfield and we ate, drank and slept the Morse code in our house for weeks! The fire service did of course swiftly become an efficient unit and the

LDV developed into the Home Guard with real uniforms and some basic equipment. It is only in very recent years that I learned of the Special Units, highly trained in sabotage with caches of arms and explosives. These units would have become very active and important in the event that we had been invaded. It still amazes me that the secret was so well kept; I don't think there was anyone at Steyning Grammar School who had any idea that the headmaster John Scragg was an active member of such a special unit (Mr and Mrs Scragg retired to live at Jolesfield House).

As kids we were always on the lookout for spies. Any stranger in the village was a potential spy and it was our job to keep an eye on them. I recall a true story of a farmer who cycled from Partridge Green to somewhere in East Sussex with a spare wireless set for his mother. He was stopped and searched and then questioned at some length before being allowed to continue with his journey. Sadly we never had such good fortune in Partridge Green as to find a stranger with a wireless.

We were in the war proper after the collapse of the British Army in France and the Dunkirk evacuation. The first we knew about it was when dirty, tired and seemingly broken soldiers came into homes in the village to have baths. As children we did not begin to understand anything that was going on nor the significance of it but even we were uplifted when Winston Churchill came on the scene with his wonderful morale-boosting speeches.

I have already mentioned rationing mainly with reference to meat. All food was, of course, rationed and every individual had a ration book giving an entitlement to no more than a few ounces of butter, sugar, cheese, etc. Clothing, coal and paraffin were also rationed. Our great suffering as children was when sweets were rationed and I can recall visiting Mrs Paris' sweet and newsagent shop with my first coupons, overlooking the fact I still had to pay for the sweets! Eventually we developed a taste for Victory Vs which were cough lozenges and not on ration.

What was the day to day evidence in the village that we were in the middle of a world war? All windows, in houses, shops and the school were crisscrossed with strips of brown paper to reduce flying glass; everyone bought special blackout material and made curtains which hung in every window; the siren would send out a two-tone wail to warn of an air raid and then a single tone to signal the all clear; church bells did not ring throughout the war as this would have signalled an invasion; there were soldiers everywhere, with large convoys moving through as well as our 'residents' at Shermanbury Grange and West Grinstead Park.

The first troops into Shermanbury Grange were a Welsh Regiment and there was a New Zealand force there early in the war, no doubt en route for France, but most of the war our 'residents' were Canadians. Another familiar sight in the late afternoon were the groups of German POWs who would collect together to be picked up for return to camp at Shipley after work on the farms and in other businesses.

There were a number of major incidents in and around the village. News of a plane that had crashed or crash-landed was always of interest and many would cycle to see a crashed plane and, hopefully be allowed near enough to collect a piece of the aircraft. Bombs could be heard to drop at night from time to time and the craters in the fields had to be visited the next day with us knowledgeable kids pontificating about whether it was a 50lb or a 100lb bomb.

It was in July 1941 when the first structural damage was caused. A Junkers 88 had been tailed by a night fighter and I remember hearing the cannon fire that shot it down. This was followed by engine noise which grew louder and louder and it crashed in the field to the south of Lock Lane, opposite Copyhold. This event changed our whole way of life from then on. We had always slept through the nights regardless of air raids but now we started getting up. I was, surprisingly, allowed to join my father and other men pacing up and down in the road (for what purpose I've no idea) while my mother sat indoors close to the cupboard under the stairs. It is difficult to believe but from Partridge Green we could frequently see a glow in the sky far to the north that we took to be the fires of London. We used to think we could recognise different plane engine noises and the words of comfort were "it's all right, it's one of ours".

The coastal defences were considerable. Whether or not the beaches were mined I do not know but we all believed they were. Along much of the coast metal structures like scaffolding were erected at the water line to make it difficult for small boats to land. We never went to the beach during the war; in fact, one had to give a reason to visit a coastal town and every time we visited my aunt in Hove we were questioned at Hove station by a policeman. We all had to carry identity cards of course; my number was ENFM.22.5. The letters denoted the area, our family was number 22 and I was number 5 in the family having 2 elder brothers. What value these cards were I do not know because they were only made of ordinary brown cardboard and must have been the easiest things in the world to forge.

Slogans – we lived with them throughout the war and afterwards for as long as food rationing continued. "Careless talk costs lives"; "Eat less bread, eat potatoes instead"; "Wings for Victory" and "Lady Churchill's Aid for Russia Fund". Also putting every available pound into National Savings. Stamps that could be bought for 6d (2½ pence) and would then be converted into a 15 shillings (75 pence) certificate which would become worth £1 after something like 7 years – about 3% compound I think. There was a sort of moral pressure on children to support this scheme.

There was one very frightening moment for the village when one lone German bomber flew low over Partridge Green. I remember hearing it while I was pumping up my bike tyres and looked up to see it directly overhead and as it went away from me I watched as the bomb doors opened and two quite small bombs were falling. He tried to hit Betley Bridge to damage the strategic 'puffing billy' railway link between Partridge Green and Henfield but missed. The village should be eternally grateful to that German airman because just before I saw it the plane had flown low along the High Street where there were lots of children on their way home from school. He could have strafed* the street or dropped his bombs there, but thankfully he chose not to.

Next came Hitler's charming V1 doodlebugs. They did not all fly that straight and they became a regular feature of the 1943 scenario. These fell when the fuel gave out so we would watch them with bated breath and breathed a sigh of relief when the popped along past us. One did fall in the village one night in the field opposite the church, just to the south of Jolesfield House.

By now the tide was turning. We had all followed the war maps in North Africa and in Russia. The names of Russian cities became all too familiar — Rostov on D Stalingrad, etc. In Africa General Montgomery (Monty) was a national hero. The build up of troops and the number of exercises in and around Partridge Green was very noticeable and finally came D-Day. We were now able to study maps of the area just across the channel and it all became very exciting. In the first few days after the Normandy landings there were quite a number of ambulances driving through, probably running between Shoreham Harbour and Horsham where hospitals nursed a great number of casualties.

My memories of the 11 months from June 1944 to Victory in Europe in May 1945 are not very clear but I well remember being allowed into a pub for a drink at the age of 15! There was a huge bonfire built in the old field to the south of South Street and Mrs DuCann managed to get some fireworks but they were so unstable we were only allowed to throw them into the fire. It was August of 1945 while on a youth week at Bognor that we learned of the atomic bombs on Japan and heard that the war was at last over.

Life slowly got back to normal but I must say that for me as a boy it never really changed all that much.

*strafe – to rake with fire at close range especially with machine-gun fire from a low flying aircraft.

School, Sport and Aircraft

Extracts from an interview with John Jones

A crowd of us used to go from Jolesfield school to the recreation ground, take a football from the school, pick two sides and play football. I was playing in defence with Bert Lander and Tony Sayers was in goal and the ball was right down the other end. They were kicking about their side of the pitch and I heard a noise of a plane, which you heard all the time during the war, and I looked over towards Partridge Green and two planes were coming very very low over us. I used to know all the planes as I used to collect the Canadian postcards with pictures of all the types and views on the back from different angles. I said to Bert Lander, "look, there's a Messerschmitt and a Focke Wolfe coming." He looked up, and I've got a feeling he didn't believe me, and as it came over so low, the chap in the Messerschmitt dipped and I looked up and could see him looking at us and I could not believe it. He came over us and all the kids started running because he went round to attack the searchlight which used to be at the bottom of the hill up on the old windmill. They attacked that with machine-gun fire and us kids, we all ran and tried to get under the pavilion. I never forgot because it was on bricks and we were trying to get under it and there was broken glass, dog muck everywhere and half of us had to give up because it was so filthy under there. Anyway, apparently I heard afterwards, it machine-gunned the searchlight battery but most of the men were down the pub as it was daylight. I don't know what damage was done. That experience was quite something, but they weren't interested in school kids. They went on from there and they shot up the train in West Grinstead station and killed the driver, and they went on up towards Horsham. All us kids were full of excitement going back to school, walking down the road, and over come seven Mustangs, Americans from Ford or Tangmere, chasing after them. What happened after that I don't know.

I remember the evacuees coming in coaches. They took over the school and us locals were put in the Methodist chapel. We were out there, we didn't have proper books or anything and it was very poor schooling. At the end of the day they didn't know what to do with you. We were allowed to take our own toys to school because they hadn't got organized then and I remember we were running around where the spiked fences were out the front and a plane came along. It was a German bomber and it was obviously in trouble and there were three planes, whether they were Spitfires or Hurricanes I don't know, but they were taking turns in having a go at this bomber as it came by right over West Grinstead. Then a Hurricane or Spitfire got just that little bit too bold and the German got him, he peeled off and came down in West Grinstead Park and I suppose the other two then sorted him out but by then it had gone out of sight. Us kids got on our bikes and went to West Grinstead Park, and as you go past the Old Tabby Cat there is a lodge house just there on the left, well it came down in that field. We were one of the first to get there. This pilot had crash landed and it was not many minutes before the army got there. I don't know how they got the information, but they seemed to know, whether they were watching or what, but that's where it came down, the Spitfire or Hurricane.

Extract from the January 1941 parish newsletter:

The Brixton school children presented a Nativity Play in Partridge Green Village Hall. Congratulations to all concerned on the beauty of the presentation. Artistically it was very satisfying. The producers cleverly divided the stage to represent heaven and earth, and the angels kept the representation most vivid. The children were both dignified and natural in their movements. The dresses were beautiful. Much care had been taken with the detail. The musical accompaniment, including the carols, brought us into the atmosphere of the Christmas story, and kept us there.

Women's Organisations

By Barbara Berry

Women's Institute (W.I.)

In the thirties the W.I. collected vegetables for the unemployed in Brighton. In the early war years there was still very high unemployment there and they continued this work. Previously they had distributed them by car, but petrol rationing made this increasingly difficult.

In January 1940 Mrs. Gumbrill started collecting books for the Red Cross and Mrs. Langton was organizing the collection of games, cards and books for the Sussex Anti-Aircraft Club. Collecting books was an important activity – 614 books were collected for the Chichester Hospital Library and scrap-books and toys were provided for the Hospital for Children in Horsham.

A Red Cross Sub-Depot was started in Partridge Green and its main function seemed to have been collecting hospital apparel for the wounded. During the first year a total of 617 articles passed through their hands, including pyjamas, shirts, dressing gowns and nightdresses. However, they had to break off from these activities for part of the year owing to an urgent order from Brighton Hospital to make 220 decontamination bags (these were in addition to the 617 articles). These were made and dispatched in three weeks.

In Dial Post a Red Cross unit was set up in readiness to deal with civilian casualties. Local people were trained with weekly lectures and practical demonstrations. A great deal of work had been done at the Guest House in bringing the Unit up to efficiency in supplies and equipment. Willing hands painted the rooms and set up clean surroundings.

In March a Miss Gilchrist demonstrated how to overcome war-time cooking problems and a fruit preservation centre was set up. As well as preserving surplus fruit and vegetables during the growing season children were encouraged to gather fruits from the hedgerows.

Both Jolesfield and Dial Post schools were feeling financial pressure with the extra numbers of evacuees and both were providing school lunches. These were basically self financing with the Government providing rations but the extra numbers were straining equipment resources. For example, the drains from the kitchens had to be enlarged. The W.I. helped raise money for these needs. It is interesting to note a report from the W.I. saying; "....the lunches are properly served and the tables properly laid."

By early 1941 goods were being collected for parcels for prisoners of war and a special committee was formed to deal with this via the Red Cross sub-depot.

In March members were urged to eat more potatoes to save bread, and Jolesfield school started a vegetable garden, which the children looked after both at school and during the holidays.

In March 1942 it was decided to organize a canning centre in the village and in 1943 toys were being collected for refugees from Malta and Gibraltar as well as for the local hospitals.

Women's Voluntary Service (W.V.S.)

With the evacuation of children from London at outbreak of war the W.V.S. were given the task of finding homes for the evacuees. Mrs. Langton was in charge of finding homes for the evacuees from Brixton school and others who arrived separately with their children from other parts of London. The evacuees were assembled in the village hall and allocated to all families that had a spare room. They tried to keep siblings together but one mother arrived with four children and Mrs. Langton took them home with her to Copyhold in Lock Lane. Few people were able to take five people in!

By 1940 the W.V.S. were supplying hot drinks to the children staying for lunch at Jolesfield school. They had a choice of hot milk, hot cocoa or Bovril for 1d (less than 0.5p) and proved very popular.

The W.V.S. also arranged a weekly collection of vegetables at "The Elms" for a minesweeper.

Working Parties for the Troops were formed and Mrs. Bernard Hornung provided three centres for collecting knitted goods for the locally based soldiers. There were weekly meetings of the Working Parties and in the first 9 months of 1940 knitted goods provided to the armed services were as follows:

Item	Royal Navy	Army
Helmets	24	9
Pairs of Steering Gloves	20	
Pairs of Socks	26	6
Pairs of Sea Boot Stockings	12	
Jerseys	18	
Cap Scarves	3	33
Pairs of Mittens		2
Pairs of Gloves		4
Cardigans		1
Scarves		4

Jumble Sales were arranged to pay for the wool needed to knit these garments.

Spam and Tea.

From the memoirs of Claire Walton

At the beginning of the war Mrs. Green of Caryllhurst in Park Lane joined the W.V.S., as did so many others. Later this was to become the Women's Royal Voluntary Service (the W.R.V.S. of today). She started a canteen for the army - with two unused huts and much hope - which had no recreational facilities locally. The canteen was situated on the north side of the A272 immediately before the Buck Barn crossroads (no traffic lights in those days).

Overnight it became very popular; at least it was somewhere for the boys to go for a cup of tea or coffee and a chat with a few locals. Mrs. Murray of Glebe Cottage (a Hornung grandchild) was Mrs. Green's deputy and together they collected various other helpers by the simple process of knocking on doors and asking for help. When I started work I could only go two evenings a week. My shift consisted of Mrs. Green and Mrs. Ken Tidey (Madge) of the Nurse's Bungalow in Park Lane (sold when new accommodation for the nurse was built next door to the headmaster's house at the former Jolesfield school). Ken was the eldest of Harry Tidey's family and was employed by Southern Railway but he and Madge wanted to get out into the country at that time with their young son. Then there was Mrs. Court, wife of a porter at West Grinstead Station, who lived in one of the Station Cottages, and me.

Mrs. Green in 1956
Courtesy of Di Holman

Evenings were enjoyable and on the whole we had a lot of fun getting to know the men and all about their families and problems and generally providing the 'tea and sympathy'.

The food consisted mainly of spam (American luncheon meat) sandwiches but I was always delegated to making the tea and coffee, so I don't remember details of the food, except that sandwich making seemed to go on forever.

Obviously there were times when supplies became difficult but nothing daunted Mrs. Green, if necessary she would fetch the provisions herself, from Horsham I suppose. She was a prominent resident of the parish, a W.W.1 widow with one son serving with the Irish Guards in W.W.2. She was not easily deflected from her task.

After the massive bombing raid on Coventry a nationwide call went out for W.V.S. helpers to go to that city at once; many emergency jobs had to be tackled. Two members of our small staff went, I never found out who they were and I was told in no uncertain terms that I was too young to go – under 21!   There was no point in arguing with that (I was really disappointed) and mother was more than a little relieved. She had plenty to worry about as my sister was training at St Mary's Hospital, Paddington, a large teaching hospital very near a main line terminus and therefore in the priority target area for German air attacks. My sister was evacuated to a large hospital in Basingstoke, Hants where their life was much quieter of course, but she had to go where she was most needed and we never knew where she went to and from for so much of the time. She was with the Royal Naval A.R.P. and had casualties from Portsmouth and Southampton.

Farming

By Dorothy Banks

Farming before the war

A combination of factors, including Governmental neglect, increased production abroad, the Depression and falling prices had left British agriculture in a poor state by the mid 1930s. About two thirds of British food consumption was supplied by imports and many farms were neglected and worked at subsistence level: described by Richard Verrall of Dial Post as "overrun with scrub, the ditches full, the soil unproductive".

By 1938 agricultural prices were still only one third above pre first world war levels and there was little incentive to invest in efficient farming. The 1937 Agriculture Act did attempt to provide incentives for increased yields by granting subsidies for improvers such as lime and slag, but as late as July 1938 Neville Chamberlain was still denying that there was a need for increased home food production. Add to this the farmers' memories — especially long when it comes to hard times — of the "Great Betrayal" of 1921, when the Government dismantled the support measures offered to farmers in World War I, and the scale of the task facing those responsible for dramatically increasing domestic food production becomes apparent. These verses, bearing a marked similarity to Kipling's poem "Tommy", would have struck a chord with many:

> Restrict him here, restrict him there, the agitating brute.
> But it's "work like blazes, farmer" when the guns begin to shoot.
>
> When U-boats sink imported foods, he's made the Nation's pet,
> Let's hope the farmer isn't fooled! Let's hope he don't forget!
> Col J Creagh-Scott (in *Farmer and Stockbreeder*)

Slag was the black, dried, and powdered scum that formed on the top of molten steel in the furnaces. It was a source of phosphates, a fertiliser which became increasingly scarce as the war advanced. It arrived on the farm in 2cwt hessian sacks. Hessian sacks were often worn across the shoulders as an extra layer of clothing by outside workers: one Land Girl working near Billingshurst wore them when working in the rain, as the coats issued to them were barely adequate.

Lime was used to reduce the natural acidity of the local clay so that it could better support arable crops.

The land is a vital war weapon

The task of encouraging farmers to increase food production was given to the War Agricultural Executive Committees (War Ags). War Ags were first formed in World War 1 and revived in time for World War II. They were organised on a County basis and members served voluntarily; Sir Merrik Burrell of Knepp was chairman of the West Sussex WAEC. On September 1st 1939 the committees were given wide powers to regulate cultivation and land management, end tenancies and take possession of land. They were responsible directly to the Ministry of Agriculture.

Every farm was surveyed and production was measured by annual returns from each farm. A detailed survey of every holding in every parish in the whole country was carried out for 1941. In West Grinstead there were some 50 holdings covering some 4600 acres, of which two thirds were less than 100 acres in size, which was considered small even then; in West Sussex as a whole, less than 40% fell into this category. However, this parish was not atypical for this part of

Sussex: Shipley, Shermanbury and Ashurst had an even greater proportion of "small" farms. Nearly half the occupiers were described as part-time or hobby farmers and over a third had been on their farms for less than 5 years (although this does not necessarily mean that they were new to farming). All but a handful, following long tradition, supported dairy or beef cattle, some supplying London. Few before the war would have produced much in the way of cash crops such as wheat: permanent grass constituted 76% of the agricultural land. In this our parish was not at all unusual; it is estimated that 88% of the nation's wheat consumption was imported before the war.

One of the first, and rather sensitive, duties of the War Ags was to visit every farm and grade not only the quality of land but also the farmer's competence. This last had three classifications: A, B and C. The inspectors were asked to give reasons for a B or C grading, such as old age, lack of capital or personal failings, and to give details of the personal failings. In West Grinstead in 1941 52% of the farms earned an A, 38% were graded as B, and 11% warranted a C grade. Compared with the Horsham District as a whole, West Grinstead had far fewer A grades and a higher proportion of B grades. Unfortunately we have found no record of any grading guidelines that may have been issued to the local inspectors, but the comments on the individual returns give some idea. B grade farmers seem to have been those who would respond to help and advice. These are some of the comments recorded:

"Lack of experience of arable farming."
"Mostly lack of confidence. He has neglected fences and ditches and failed to use fertilizers apart from dung. He is yielding to persuasion and improving."
"Knows nothing of farming. Employs bailiff who does not understand plant requirements. Will probably succeed with advice."
"There is sound knowledge but labour is short, and fences and ditches are not as they should be. He is but little short of A standard."
"Fails to appreciate the value of phosphates. Is quite efficient in other respects."
"Not a very hard worker and untidy"

The few (5) C graded farms elicited the following comments:
"No knowledge. No initiative. No ambition or energy."
"Lack of capital"
"Not practical"
"'Gentleman Farmer'. Investments seriously affected by the war. Practical experience of farming in general very limited"
"Mostly works for other farmers and pays insufficient attention to his own holding"

Some of these C farms were obviously badly neglected, as defined by these wartime standards. The condition of the pasture and arable land (if there was any) was described as poor or bad, with little or no use of fertilisers and infested with rabbits, rooks and wood pigeons, insects and weeds. General amenability of the occupier may also have played a part in the judgment. It was not unusual for such farms to be requisitioned by the War Ags, but we know of none suffering such a fate in this parish.

Of course, mechanisation was in its infancy. Tractor ownership was restricted to 17 farms even by 1941 (although Needs and Tuckmans farms had two!), most of the work was done with horses, and, of course, many of the cows were milked by hand. Less than half the farmhouses had electricity, and less than a quarter had power on the farm.

All this formed the background to the triple challenge of how to compensate for drastically reduced imports of animal feedstuffs without loss of milk and meat yield, whilst at the same time increasing production of crops for human consumption – and, on top of all this, keeping soil fertility at a level sufficient to support the demands of a long war.

The problems facing this part of Sussex are described by Sir Merrik Burrell, himself a farmer at Floodgates, writing in the Royal Agricultural Society for England's journal in May 1942:

"*Wealden clay, heavy and wet, short of phosphates, very difficult and costly to handle as arable, divided into small farms and small fields. When the war started some 50% of these farms had not got one acre of arable, and consequently no arable implements and little knowledge on the part of the farmers as to arable cultivation. It had gradually been given up to milk production based on home grown hay and purchased cheap imported feeding stuffs. The problem here has been to plough up and get sufficiently well cultivated an area on each farm on which to grow feeding stuffs for the cows. It is not suitable land for spring crops. Besides milk, wheat is in war-time the only important cash crop produced in the Weald.*"

Ploughing of farms is as vital as arms

The farmers of West Grinstead (and the rest of the country) rose to the task.

Under the famous ploughing up campaigns, the number of acres producing cereal crops on local farms more than tripled between 1939 and 1944 from 400 acres to 1200 acres. Acreage under crops grown purely for fodder more than doubled, from 140 to 290 acres in the same period. Even the number of beef and dairy cattle rose.

The amount of land classified as "rough grazings" – ie ground given over to game shooting, deer parks, or fields that habitually flooded etc – fell from 444 acres in 1939 to 106 acres in 1944, partly, no doubt, as a result of the deer park at West Grinstead Park being put to the plough in 1942, but also as the military presence increased.

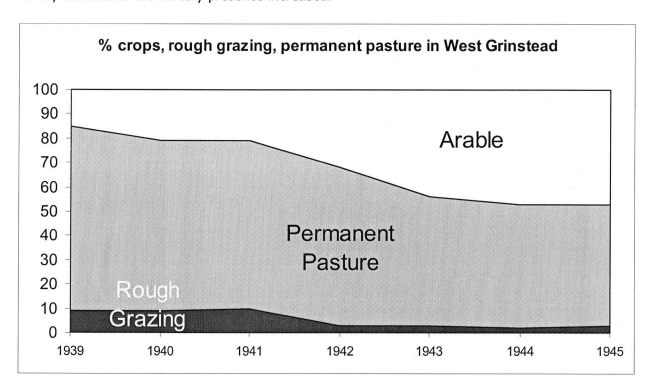

Source: National Archives MAF 68

However, the number of sheep recorded plummeted – by 1941 only Rookland Farm (now part of the Lock Estate) had a significant flock. As was the case in the rest of the country, commercial pig and poultry stocks also fell, as they competed inefficiently for food edible by humans. However, the numbers of poultry kept by non-farming households undoubtedly increased at the same time, and there might have been the odd pig or two that escaped official recognition.

All this was done while the military occupied increasing amounts of land and, as one County War Ag. committee member put it, farmers "*ditched and drained tens of thousands of acres, increased the supply of milk and grown at home the majority of food for their livestock, and undertook a score of other activities they would not have dreamt of before the War. More amazing still, they have managed to fill up, without exaggeration, at least ten times the number of forms that even they were accustomed to; nearly every form at least twice as diabolical as any invented by Government Departments before the War".* (RASE Journal 1942)

Pothill Farm is a good example of the effects of the ploughing up campaign in just the first two years of the war. In 1941 the owner had been in possession for just one year; the farm was given a B rating on account of his inexperience, but the farmer was described as "keen and very anxious for success". The grassland ploughed in those first two years totalled 38 acres, which represented a quarter of the total. The farm supported in addition 61 cattle, of which 25 were cows in milk.

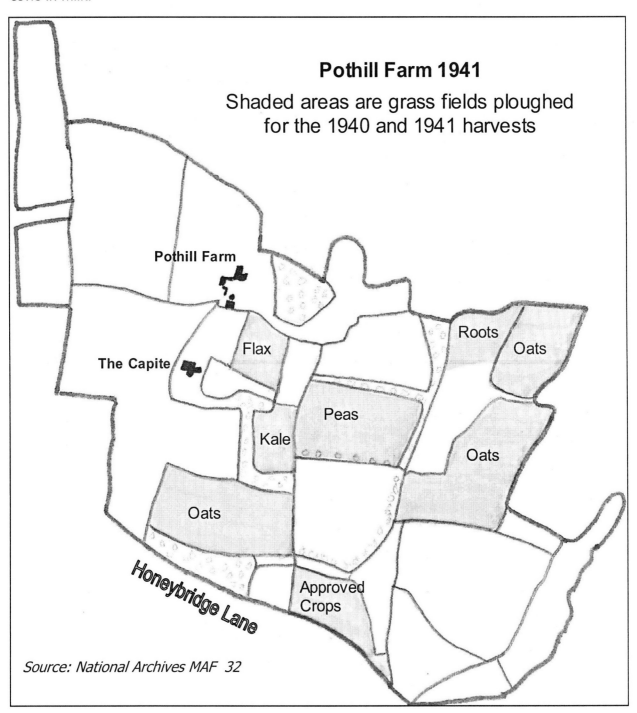

Pothill Farm 1941

Shaded areas are grass fields ploughed for the 1940 and 1941 harvests

Pothill Farm

The Capite

Flax

Roots

Oats

Peas

Kale

Oats

Oats

Honeybridge Lane

Approved Crops

Source: National Archives MAF 32

The transformation in land use and types of farming brought about by the war, as reported in the Annual Farm Survey returns, is summarised in the table below.

The doubling of the acreage under cereal crops in the first two years of the war is testament to the success of the ploughing up campaigns administered by the WAEC. The number of acres put to wheat production peaked in 1943, a phenomenon repeated across the country; this was a deliberate policy by the Government caused by the growing success in 1941 and 1942 of the enemy U-boat campaign. Wheat production fell after that, partly because greater emphasis was placed on producing feed crops for livestock and also partly because the dash for cash crops of the early years was putting soil fertility at risk. The growing importance of leguminous crops (such as clover, sainfoin and lucerne), which return nitrogen to the soil through their roots, was designed to mitigate that.

Crops in W Grinstead (acres)	1939	1940	1941	1942	1943	1944	1945
Wheat	186	172	355	353	637	609	422
Oats	197	301	279	323	389	508	469
Other cereals	14	75	158	116	115	87	153
Total cereals	**397**	**548**	**792**	**792**	**1141**	**1204**	**1044**
Fodder only crops	142	140	176	249	288	284	282
Potatoes	4	6	14	9	16	22	28
Flax	0	17	56	44	22	36	40
Bare fallow	77	80	8	81	93	91	69
Clover/sainfoin/lucerne etc	76	176	119	205	263	345	643
Permanent grass	3560	3227	2864	2769	2208	2252	2143
Rough grazings	444	385	421	122	105	106	116
Cattle	**1252**	**1260**	**1349**	**1370**	**1430**	**1452**	**1389**
Pigs	**313**	**373**	**248**	**83**	**68**	**82**	**137**
Sheep	**256**	**511**	**233**	**215**	**149**	**160**	**229**
Poultry	**5421**	**5739**	**4803**	**3788**	**3047**	**3008**	**3328**

Source: National Archives MAF 68

The price of this tripling of arable acreage was the collapse (locally and nationally) of pig and poultry stocks particularly, but also of sheep numbers. Milk production remained a national priority, but struggled to maintain pre-war levels (the fact that cattle numbers did not fall here in West Grinstead does not necessarily mean that milk and beef yields did not); indeed some farmers in some areas of England and Wales who had dropped out of milk, discovering that arable was more profitable and less arduous, were "encouraged" to return in 1943, when serious shortages threatened.

Of course, the need to continue to feed the nation did not recede with the ceasefire, and rationing famously continued for many years afterwards. The Sussex WEAC was not disbanded until 1949.

Approved crops

Throughout the war, the Ministry of Agriculture issued to each County WAEC targets of acres that should be laid to certain crops, known as approved crops. This meant that no farm escaped being subject to "Cultivation Orders" which were issued by the War Ags on a weekly basis. These orders were "to plough, prepare and sow in a husbandlike manner with one of the approved crops" that included wheat, oats, barley, rye, mixed corn, peas, beans, potatoes and sugar beet, for the harvest of each given year. The relative importance of these crops would change according to the success (or losses) of imports as the war progressed, but the most "important" crops remained wheat and potatoes.

Farmers here concentrated in the main on proven crops (wheat and oats) known to have some chance on the local heavy soil. Potato production did increase sevenfold but still formed a tiny proportion (1%) of the cultivated total. However, flax, which was virtually unheard of before the war, was introduced with continuing success in 1940. In 1941 the biggest growers of flax were Glebe Farm and Lloyts Farm.

Carrots and sticks

The War Ags adopted the principle that persuasion and incentives would yield better results in increasing production than compulsion. Prices for crops and produce were guaranteed (not always to everybody's satisfaction), and farmers were awarded £2 for every acre of pasture ploughed to plant approved crops. Practical help and advice were available from the War Ag members. However, compulsion sometimes became necessary: the West Sussex County Times records two West Grinstead farmers being fined £5 each for failing to comply with ploughing orders in 1941, and a farm near Dial Post was requisitioned, the occupiers being evicted. There is evidence that at least two farm occupiers in West Grinstead (one a tenant of the Knepp Estate and one of the West Grinstead Park Estate) were "leant on" quite hard by the local War Ag. to comply with its wishes.

Trawlers Farm in Shipley, where the land had been kept for rough shooting since 1922, would therefore have earned a 'C' rating by the War Ag. The farm was requisitioned and run by the War Ag. for the duration of the war, and returned to its owners afterwards. Shermanbury Park, just to the east of "our patch", was also taken over by the War Ag, some of the land being farmed by Herbert Mitchell. Shermanbury Grange itself was requisitioned for Canadian troops.

By October 1943 the WAEC for West Sussex had requisitioned 122 "lots", with a total area of 6,593 acres. Of this, 1,337 acres had been let, 611 acres had been taken over by the Military and 488 acres had been "deregulated". This left 4,157 acres, spread over 78 owners or occupiers, that the Committee still had in hand. However, it is unclear whether, or how much of this land was actually put to any "good" use in the course of the war, as making it productive often involved many logistical difficulties.

The War Agricultural Executive Committee

The War Agricultural Executive Committee met every week, co-ordinating the work of the four district sub-committees whose members were drawn from "some of the best farmers in the area". The Horsham District sub-committee included locally Charles Limbrick (bailiff to the Knepp Estate), George Verrall (Thistleworth Farm), Albert Smith (Pollards Hill Farm), Tommy Thornton (New Barn Farm, Dial Post), Mr Webley, Mr Capsey and Mr Robinson at Woodmans.

The WAEC produced a weekly bulletin, whose content ranged over latest fixed prices for produce and crops, logistical difficulties, pest control, wages, clothing, rations for chick rearing, rules for military service, allotment of equipment etc.

Nearly every week, space was given over to their directives in the local newspapers under slogans such as "Plough Now", "Ploughing on Farms is as Vital as Arms" and "Increase the Yield of all your Fields".

From the W Sussex WAEC members' bulletin:

13.11.41: Domestic poultry keepers cannot at present be allowed permits to purchase wire netting.

11.12.41: As from 15th December agricultural workers will receive 12 ounces of cheese a week instead of 8 ounces.

22.1.42: The Ministry has announced that as an experiment a number of "good conduct" Italian prisoners would be permitted to "live in" on farms and work for individual farmers. It appears that unauthorised statements may have given the impression that farmers will be compelled to take these prisoners and the Ministry wishes to make it clear that this is not the case.

4.6.42: A limited quantity of reconditioned battle dresses has been made available for agricultural workers and farmers. The dresses are dyed dark green and the retail price will be 21/-. They will be sold coupon free.

7.1.43: Persons engaged in agriculture may obtain a thermos flask from any retailer for 4½d (certificate required).

The WAEC organised training sessions for farmers unused to arable farming, and co-ordinated the work of the labour gangs (one was billeted at Brinsbury House), whose work included land drainage and ploughing on farms unable or unwilling to do it themselves. They approved financial loans for seed and manures to under-capitalised farmers. Sir Merrik Burrell summed up the role of the Executive Committee: "(it) has no wish to drive and to bully, nor to interfere unduly, but desires only to lead, inspire, and assist every occupier to produce the utmost from his farm."

Whatever the policy, it was undeniably hands-on, and a reading of the committees' minutes reveals that not all was sweetness and light all the time, especially in the first couple of years. Almost every detail of farming was controlled by the War Ag; even A grade farmers had to have their crop or cultivation proposals approved, and this clearly proved difficult to swallow by some farmers.

Fertilisers were rationed, tyres were rationed in 1942 — a rationed commodity was at least one that could be relied upon. But as the war progressed so shortages of essential products increased. In Richard Verrall's words: "The War Ag controlled the distribution of all machinery and materials, so if something was allocated, or became available, you took it, even if you did not need it when it arrived."

One thing farmers did have regular access to was petrol (as well as agricultural fuel): 3 gallons a week for one local farm. This may have made them very popular with their neighbours, but woe betide anybody who was caught in a car not on official business! As Bette Sawyer of Dial Post recalls: "Right through the war a friend from Shipley — Harold Johnson — and I organised and ran concerts for the British Red Cross and we raised a lot of money, but we did have problems. If we were rehearsing a play or similar, sometimes someone couldn't come because they were on duty, fire watching, Home Guard etc, but we got there in the end. Another problem we had was transport as petrol was rationed and one had to have a good reason for being out in the car at night. Quite often it had to be an urgent trip to get something from the vet."

Farmers (and the War Ags themselves) were flooded with endless directives, orders and advice. Of the many hundreds produced, here is a personal favourite, from 1942.

4.   Rubber Boots

        The Minister of Agriculture has informed Executive
Committees that from his personal observation he feels that
the gravity of the rubber situation may not be fully appreciated
by the farming community, since rubber boots are still being
worn when neither weather conditions nor the type of work
involved justifies their use.
        Only a very small proportion of the applicants to
the Committee for permits to purchase rubber boots can be
supplied.
        Committees are instructed not to issue buying permits
to farmers if there are already sufficient rubber boots on the
farm, whether owned by the farmer or his workers; nor should
permits be issued to individuals unless the Committee are
convinced that rubber boots are essential for the performance of
the work for which they are required. In the case of replacements the Committee should satisfy themselves that the
applicant has taken steps to ascertain whether the boots can
be repaired, and if beyond repair, a reasonable explanation
should be furnished as to why the boots were allowed to reach
such a condition.

Rabbits, rats and rooks

Pest control became an important part of the food production strategy. Advertisements went into the County Times appealing for "skilled vermin destroyers, including mole catchers, rabbit catchers, and rat catchers" in 1940 and the War Ags. were given authority to serve rabbit, rook, rat and pigeon orders compelling farmers to reduce the pests or to enter the land with their own catchers. In 1943 the sparrow joined the list of undesirables:

The Ministry of Agriculture consider it imperative to take all possible steps to reduce the number of house sparrows. Farmers should be urged to destroy house sparrows' nests, eggs or young and to set sparrow traps when the young birds leave the nest. Great care should be taken to ensure that nests/eggs/birds such as hedge sparrow and chaffinch (which are beneficial to agriculture) are not destroyed by mistake.

West Sussex Agricultural Executive Committee minutes, 8th April 1943

This tactic was so successful that by 1941 it was estimated that one million tons of food and feedstuffs had been saved nationally by pest control alone. Nevertheless the campaign continued throughout the war and beyond, and many a trophy skin or tail was handed in for a cash reward. Joy Gibson remembers that evidence of where Ralph and Bill Morley (workers on Dunstans Farm, and heavy smokers) had been rabbiting was easily provided by the presence of empty Woodbine cigarette packets stuffed down the holes.

The Fordson tractor

The potential of tractors on farms began to be recognised in the first World War. However, nationally, there were only 1.8 tractors per 1000 acres in 1937. The tractors available in the 1920s had lots of starting and lubrication problems. The introduction of the Fordson Model N transformed all that, although they were very primitive vehicles by today's standards. By 1940 some 50,000 had been delivered around the country since the start of the war. By 1941, there were 4 tractors per 1000 acres in West Grinstead. Every one of them a Fordson, except at Needs Farm, where Mr Beck, acknowledged as a progressive (A grade) farmer, had two Internationals.

The Fordsons were originally yellow, but it was decided that they would present too easy a target for enemy planes, so war-time tractors were painted green.

Implements of all kinds became very scarce in the war, and prices at farm sales rose substantially. There was a great deal of sharing of equipment between farmers as a result, and the War Ag. had depots of equipment for hire at Steyning, Horsham and Brinsbury.

Fordson with Bamford mower attached at Thistleworth Farm. Note the rubber tyres: these were an innovation at the start of the war, but as rubber shortages increased, so farmers were urged to revert to metal rims when the tyres needed replacing.

Courtesy of Richard Verrall

Lister Blackstone 12' hay rake at Thistleworth Farm; farmhouse in the background

Courtesy of Richard Verrall

Rick building at Thistleworth Farm with an elevator from Carter Bros of Billingshurst and Ruston engine

Courtesy of Richard Verrall

Lend a hand on the land

Agricultural workers were in a reserved occupation and were therefore not subject to obligatory call up. Nevertheless, the drive to increase production was tempered by an acute shortage of labour, as young men chose either to go into the Forces or to get better pay in other areas of War Work. As the acreage under cultivation increased, so the need for labour at crucial times grew. The official records suggest that the total agricultural work force in West Grinstead remained virtually unchanged through most of the war years, but the figures do not reflect the immensely long hours that the farmers put in, and it is generally acknowledged that they underestimate the number of Land Army girls employed. Farmers were even encouraged to fit lamps to their tractors and to plough by night as well as by day.

The Women's Land Army was organised locally from 8 Worthing Road in Horsham under Mrs Forbes-Adams, and the women were either billeted with a farm or trucked daily to wherever they were needed. Lack of suitable accommodation made things more difficult for the Land Army – many houses were already full with evacuees or members of the Forces.

By the end of September 1939 West Sussex already had 53 Land Girls placed in work. One of those was Judy Thomas, recently returned from finishing school in Switzerland and now suddenly in rather different circumstances in a cowman's hut near Billingshurst, carting sugar beet for an unhelpful farmer who held no truck with girls on the land. She was able to extricate herself when she was expected to do all the housework as well. She later moved to a much more appreciative farm, and eventually married a farmer.

Schoolchildren were encouraged to help out on the farms in the school holidays. The local Girl Guide Troup played their part by weeding bean fields. The money raised was contributed to the Baden-Powell Fund.

From 1942 prisoners of war were also used. Doug Pennifold remembers that an Italian worked at his father's wheelwright's business; the POWs would wait at the end of Lock Lane for the lorry to take them back to the Billingshurst camp at the end of the day. It was not long before POWs were living in on some farms.

Richard Verrall remembers German POWs at Thistleworth Farm: "The War Ag. allocated German POWs and they did

Miss Muriel Merritt of Partridge Green, in Land Army uniform. Taken in 1940 by Marjorie Baker.
Courtesy of Henfield Museum

32

much sterling work, harvesting, clearing, ditching and so on. I remember these Fearsome Creatures arriving in a lorry in the morning, in the secure care of one Private Pike look-a-like, who would probably have had trouble with a difficult sheep, and they worked away without any trouble or attempted escapes, as far as I know, and went home again at night to the camp at Billingshurst. The most trustworthy were billeted on farms; we had a young man named Heinz, a farmer's son, who lived in his own well set up hut. I remember he always had Sunday Dinner with us as part of the family. After the war he returned home, and wrote regularly to Mother, but as he was in the Russian Sector, the letters stopped."

Cecil Longhurst also recalls their resourcefulness: "There wasn't much point in the prisoners not being helpful, not much good trying to get away, they'd have to get across the channel and that if they did. When they were hired, the farmers would give them a meal which was often better than they'd get at camp. They made bits and pieces out of whatever they could get hold of: slippers out of sacks, reusing the unpicked threads to stitch shoes that could've come from a shop. One combed horses' manes and tails to get hair to make brushes. There were one or two that would cause trouble, maybe planting stones instead of seeds, but most of them knew it was best to keep their heads down really."

By 1943 the "lend a hand on the land" movement had policemen, Home Guard and civilians of all sorts contributing, especially at harvest and threshing times – one of the perks was being allowed to glean grain from the harvested fields for domestic chickens.

Thistleworth Farm 1943

On George Verrall's farm there were 24 dairy cows in 1943. They were milked by hand and there was no electricity. Water came from wells.

Mr Verrall's notes for the threshing of that summer record the use of 4 land girls for 54 hours at 1s 3d an hour, as well as 13½ hours of Darkie's time. Darkie was the man who did most of the hard work for the threshing gang that moved from farm to farm, getting up at 4am to get the steam up on the engine. He cost 1s 6d an hour. (Certainly before the war, the arrival of the threshing gang used to coincide with the arrival of Harris's circus). Local war evacuees were also employed on a casual basis. Later in the year Mr Verrall records the employment of POWs at 1s an hour, and the 4 land girls came back in December.

George and Phil Verrall of Thistleworth Farm, with boy Richard at the window, ready to go to market on a Wednesday during the war, with their Austin 18.
Courtesy of Richard Verrall

Thistleworth received a ploughing grant of £29 that year, equating to 14½ acres of grassland being ploughed up. This was a one-off payment from the War Ag, and could be the culmination of up to three years of improving the grassland by liming, slagging and ley-farming (fields alternating crop and fallow).

For the first time Thistleworth grew potatoes (a very desirable crop as far as the WAEC was concerned), receiving a 10s subsidy to do so.

The Estates and their owners

According to the 1941 Farm Survey nearly three quarters of local farmland was held by three largely tenanted estates: the West Grinstead Park Estate, the Lock Estate (owned by the Harvey family) and the Knepp Estate (under the Burrell family). Most of the Knepp Estate lay in Shipley, with only significant holdings at Swallows Farm and New Barn Farm in Dial Post in this parish.

As well as being chairman of the West Sussex War Agricultural Executive Committee Sir Merrik Burrell Bt CBE, (1877-1957) one-time owner of the Knepp Estate, was President of the Royal Agricultural Society for England (RASE) and Chairman of the Royal Veterinary College, and was awarded the RASE Gold Medal in 1938. He was, in short, a figure of national status in agricultural circles.

Having inherited the estate at the turn of the century, he led what could be regarded as the typical life of the country squire, including hunting four days a week, but he was also an agricultural pioneer in methods of pasture improvement as well as animal health and breeding.

Much of the eastern part of estate, known as the West Grinstead Park Estate, had been sold to the Hornung family in 1913, so by World War 2 most of the Knepp Estate lay in Shipley, having been made over to Sir Merrik's son Walter. Knepp Castle itself was occupied by the military from early on in the war, and Sir Merrik Burrell moved with his wife to Floodgates Farm for the duration.

Sir Merrik R Burrell, Bt., C.B.E.
(1877-1957)
Courtesy of RASE

Whilst much has been written about Sir Merrik's considerable achievements in adult life, Julie Beck's compilation of Cecil Longhurst's memoirs relates the story of a different sort of award when Sir Merrik was a boy: Cecil's grandfather (Mr Turrell) "worked at Floodgates, and when Sir Merrik and his sister were children they often came to Floodgates looking round the farm. One day somebody had left a ladder up to the straw rick. The roof of the straw rick was thatch, but they were having quite a game sliding down the roof which wasn't helping the thatch very much and my grandfather told them to stop it. The little girl did, but Merrik said it was his father's rick and he'd slide down it if he wanted. My grandfather said he'd box his ears if he done it again. Well, he climbed up the ladder and slid down again, so he boxed his ears. Course Merrik was rather indignant about it and they went off home. I think my grandfather was a little apprehensive about whether he ought to have gone quite so far." Many years later he heard from Miss Burrell that on the way home Merrik had said "he was going to see father and Turrell would get into trouble. As soon as they got back to the Castle they went into their father's study and Merrik said Turrell had boxed his ears. The first thing his father asked was what had they been doing? Merrik said they had been sliding down the straw rick, and his father said: 'Well I should think Turrell would box your ears and you ought to have known better'. Miss Burrell said they had to go to bed without any tea and Merrik wished he hadn't said anything about it!"

The West Grinstead Park Estate dominated this parish, with some 14 tenanted farms covering more than 2200 acres, stretching, broadly speaking, east of the A24 from Tuckmans in the north to Thistleworth and Sands in the south, and including The Kennels, Clothalls, Fosters, Needs, Rookland, Rook Cross, Gateland and Small Ham. At its centre lay West Grinstead Park House, which was occupied by the military from 1940 - an experience from which the house never recovered: it was demolished in the 1960s.

The estate had been bought in 1913 from Sir Merrik Burrell by J P Hornung, described in the West Sussex County Times as "a breeder of race horses and sugar industry pioneer". Some of the estate passed to his four children on his death in 1940, but most was bought by Ernest Edward Cook (grandson of Thomas Cook, the travel agent) and was administered by agents for the duration of the war.

J P Hornung was the elder brother of E W Hornung, who wrote the Raffles stories and married the sister of Sir Arthur Conan Doyle, whose mother had also lived in West Grinstead. This is the obituary published in the County Times:

Adventurous life in East Africa

Sussex has lost a well-known and appreciated personality by the death on Monday at his Sussex estate, West Grinstead Park, of **Mr John Peter Hornung JP.** Mr Hornung was born on June 3, 1861, and was the second son of Mr John Peter Hornung. He was educated at Edinburgh. In 1884 he married Laura, daughter of Mr J de Paiva Rapozo, of Lisbon, and he and his wife came to West Grinstead Park in 1912 (sic).

Since settling in the county he had interested himself greatly in the activities of the district. For a number of years he was President of the Horsham Hospital, and he was a Committee member of the Crawley and Horsham Hunt. He also took an active interest in the Sussex Agricultural Society, the West Grinstead Agricultural and Ploughing Match Society and the Horsham and Worthing Division of the Conservative Association.

His chief recreations were hunting, shooting and racing, and he maintained a stud farm at West Grinstead. His stallion is Papyrus, a Derby winner, and among the many famous race horses that he has bred there is Dubonnet, winner of last year's Goodwood Cup.

Much emphasis has been placed upon the sporting aspect of Mr Hornung's life, but such emphasis is unjustifiable. His life's work and greatest interest was the sugar industry, which he established more than 50 years ago in Portuguese East Africa. In that industry, now employing more than 20,000 persons, he was the guiding spirit, and up to the very last he took the keenest interest in every detail of the business. His death will be felt deeply, not only by his family and intimate circle of friends, but also by the great army of employees, at home and abroad, whose respect, loyalty and friendship he had won.

He went to East Africa in 1888 when the land surrounding the lower reaches of the Zambesi river was practically uncultivated. He spent many months alone there and realised the great potentialities of the wild country. But that realisation would not have been sufficient had he not had the courage and conviction to carry his plans through.

This courage made itself apparent on many thrilling occasions but it will suffice to cite one. To start the first sugar factory which he established in the colony he had to transport all the machinery single-handed in a native canoe, up 150 miles of crocodile infested river.

Mr Hornung leaves a widow, two sons and two daughters. He had one other son who fell in action in 1916.

West Sussex County Times of February 9th 1940

The Lock Estate, owned by Mr Andrew Harvey, controlled nearly 1300 acres (some of which lay in what was then Ashurst parish), and comprised Lock Farm, Hobshorts, Lloyts and Moat (previously and now once again Priors Byne Farm). The Harveys came to Lock House in the 1930s. Miss Diane was distinguished by being the first of Donald Campbell's three wives.

Lock Farm 1944. Mr Harvey (right) with farm manager George Jesse (centre) and Mr Harvey's stepdaughter Pat. Note the height of the corn (modern varieties are much shorter), and the patches on Mr Harvey's trousers — proof, perhaps, that nobody escaped the clothing ration.

Courtesy of Henfield Museum

And some things never change...

One of the problems encountered by the War Ags was "the effect on the efforts of all engaged on production of primary products of the unnecessary and harmful intervention of the Ministry of Food into the realm of the Ministry of Agriculture. No one denies that the Nation has been wonderfully fed and its general health maintained. But there has been a lamentable inability on the part of the Ministry of Food to understand the problems of the home producer, or indeed of the countryside generally. Cumbersome attempts on the part of the Minister of Food to make good schemes better, his interference in price fixing, and the production of inelastic regulations as to the collection and distribution of perishable articles, such as eggs and vegetables, has led to delays, lower production, serious wastage, disappointments and intense irritations. The Ministry of Agriculture with its close link with the land could never have made the mistakes caused by the apparently completely urban mind of the Ministry of Food"

Sir Merrik Burrell, writing in the RASE Journal, May 1942

Wartime Memories from Needs Farm

By Julie Beck

In September 1939 when the Second World War broke out W Beck & Son were at Needs Farm, some 272 acres to the north-west of Partridge Green. It was tenanted like some other farms around the area from the Hornungs at West Grinstead Park.

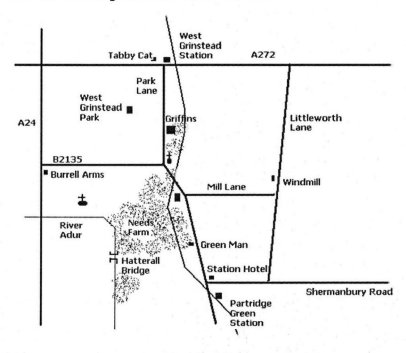

The Beck family had come to Needs from a farm in Battle at the end of 1926. The family had spent WW1 farming on the north Kent Downs and had experienced farming through wartime before.

Shorthorn cow and calves outside the south elevation of Needs, circa 1940

Producing primarily milk which would be transported by train to whichever dairy was paying the best price to process the milk, the farm was home to about 40 shorthorn cows, the entry in a Shorthorn Society Handbook of that time shows 40 cows and heifers registered with names such as Beauty, Dumpling, Frosty, Marchioness, Smutty and Wild Queen.

Medals for highest shorthorn herd average (ie milk yield) in West Sussex 1944 - 45 and 1945 – 46, with Fred Monnery, Louis Beck and George Stenning outside Needs, Louis holding the cup awarded with the medals.

1. Tractor. with extra wheels	180	
1. Tractor	100	
1. Thresher	100	
1. 3 furrow plough	45	
1. New disc harrow	47	5
1. Cultivator	15	
1. Drill	10	
3. Rollers	20	
1. Manure drill	20	
4. Sets harrows	12	
1. Chain harrow	3	
2. Horse ploughs	6	
1. Phos drill	27	15
1. Binder	90	

The inventory (above) for 1942 shows both tractors and horses being used on the farm; two tractors valued at £180 and £100 respectively, and three horses valued at £30 each plus a couple of colts.   There was a three furrow plough as well as two horse ploughs, and a power mower as well as a horse mower.

Crops produced from the land included hay, straw and corn. Mangels, a root crop like turnips, were grown to feed the cattle. Other feeds were bought in from local merchants including H J Tidey Steam Mills, Partridge Green and Prewett Stone Mills, Horsham.

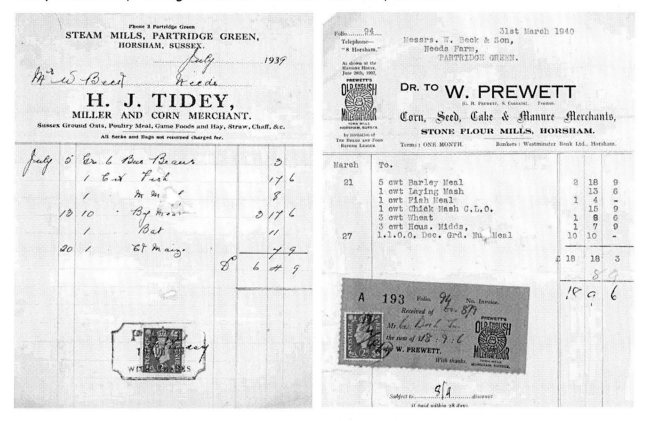

Cattle, horse and pig feed came in the guise of many: flaked maize, beet pulp, Guinness grains, fish meal and ground nut meal. Also bought in were supplies for the chicken (interestingly not mentioned in the inventory); laying mash and chick mash.

Pepper & Son at Amberley provided lime at £8 3s 6d for 6 tons divided into 120 paper bags which would probably last a couple of seasons. The lime was used to correct the acidity of the soil so they could grow crops such as barley.

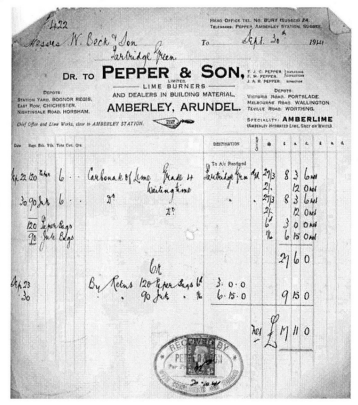

Interestingly we hear of pastures being ploughed up for the war effort, but an invoice from Miln & Co, Agricultural & Horticultural Seed Merchants from Chester suggests that in some cases pasture was being sown; 2 sacks of Milns No. 4 N E Mixture for Permanent Pasture to cover 6 acres.

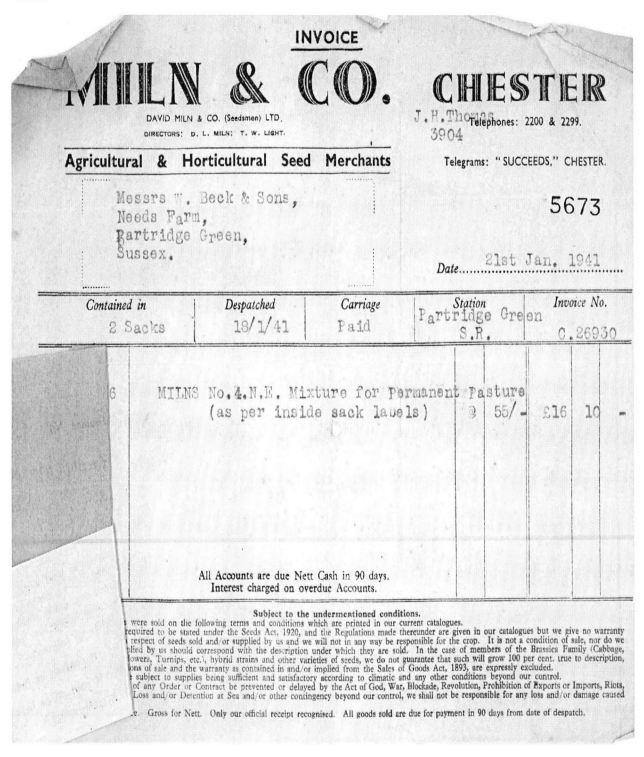

In 1940 one acre of grass field was turned to kale under W A E C's (War Agricultural Executive Committee, set up by the Ministry of Agriculture to co-ordinate food and feed production during the war) direction and 12½ acres turned to 'approved' crops in 1941. These approved crops, determined by the W A E C, could have included wheat, oats, barley, rye, mixed corn, peas or beans for stock feeding, potatoes or sugar beet. In fact, the 1941 Farm Survey records Needs as growing 58 acres of wheat, barley and oats, as well as over 20 acres of fodder crops such as beans, turnips, mangolds and kale. There were also 3 acres of flax, a relatively 'new' crop needed for textile production.

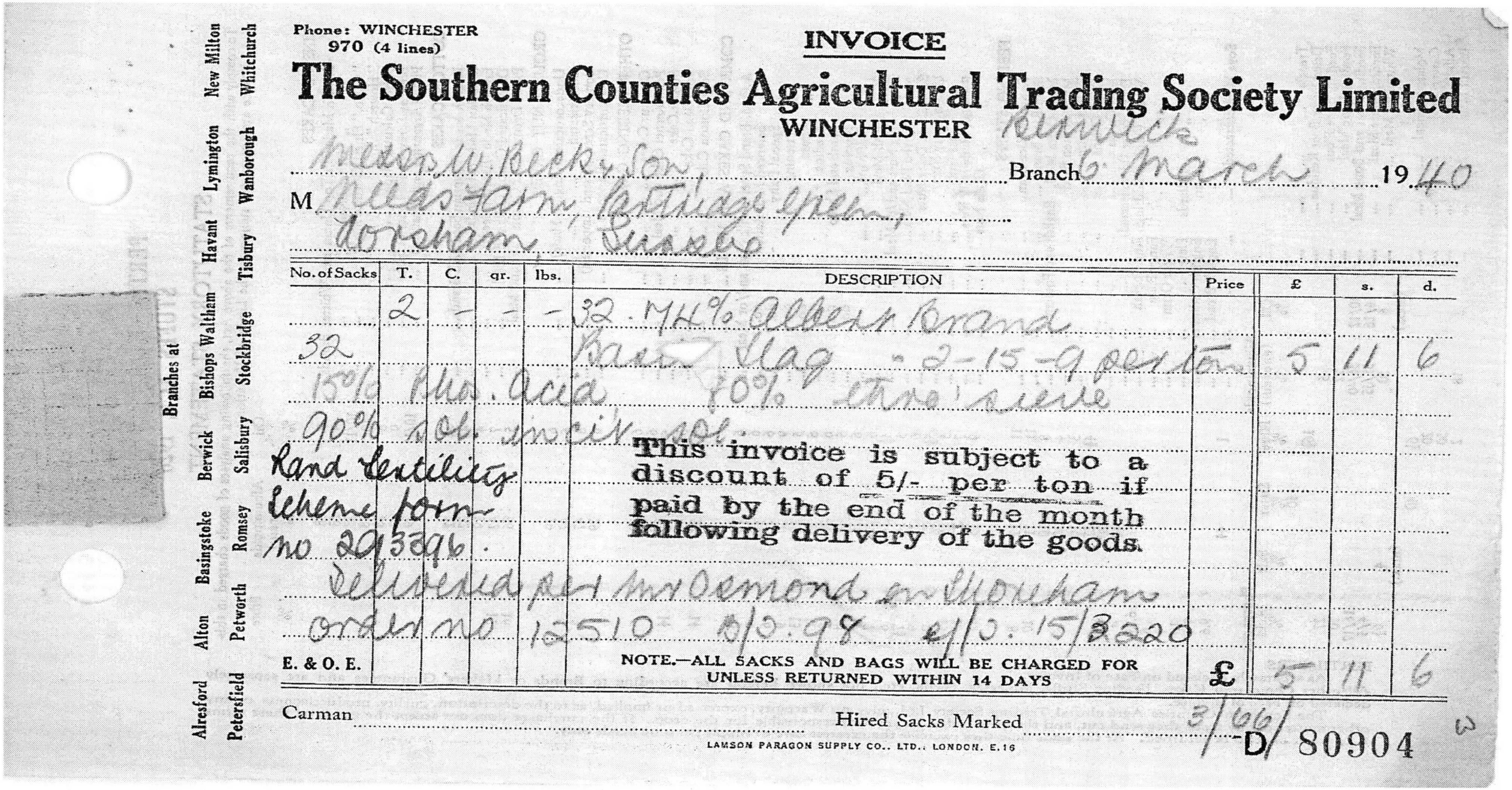

INVOICE

The Southern Counties Agricultural Trading Society Limited

WINCHESTER

Phone: WINCHESTER
970 (4 lines)

Branch. *Whitwle* .... *March* 19 4 0

M .... *Messrs. W. Dickson* ....
.... *Mitcham, Bishops Sutton,* .....
.... *Arlesford Hants* ....

No. of Sacks	T.	C.	qr.	lbs.	DESCRIPTION	Price	£	s.	d.
	2	1	1	32	*Mr 4% Basic Brand*				
					Basic Slag "-2-15-9 per ton	*2-15-9 per ton*	5	11	6
32					*15% Phos. Acid* 70% fine value				
					90% fine value				
					Land fertility scheme form no. 295896				
					Delivered to movement in Upham				
					Order no. 157510 "-8/0.9" £1/0.15/3620				

This invoice is subject to a
discount of 5/- per ton if
paid by the end of the month
following delivery of the goods.

E. & O. E. £ 5 11 6

Carman ....

Hired Sacks Marked

NOTE.—ALL SACKS AND BAGS WILL BE CHARGED FOR
UNLESS RETURNED WITHIN 14 DAYS

LAMSON PARAGON SUPPLY CO.. LTD.. LONDON. E.16

---D/ 80904

3/06/

3

Branches at:

Alresford Alton Basingstoke Berwick Bishops Waltham Havant Lymington New Milton
Petersfield Petworth Romsey Salisbury Stockbridge Tisbury Wanborough Whitchurch

Another merchant used regularly by the farm for seeds, feed and other items was The Southern Counties Agricultural Trading Society Limited (SCATS). This invoice for March 1940 shows two tons of slag being brought in under the 'land fertility scheme' and details of the acidity are supplied in the bill.

Although grass crops were grown in 1941 one ton of hay was bought from Wilcox & Frost at Chichester at a price of about £7 a ton. Bear in mind a cow was valued at £32 and could eat quite considerably more than that in a year to produce 1000 gallons of milk.

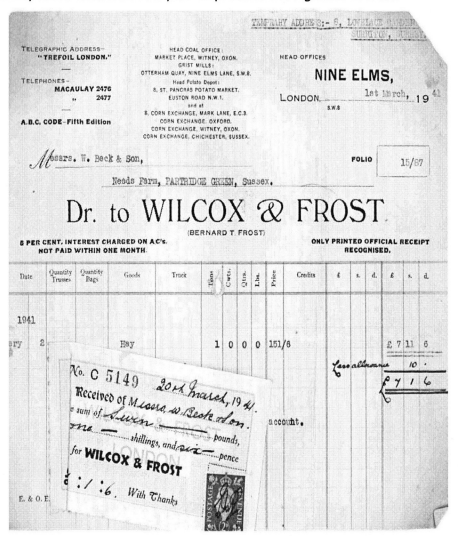

Incidentals like fuel were purchased locally. Five gallons of paraffin were bought from W J Worsfold, Motor & Cycle Engineer for 6 shillings and 3 pence (31p). On the same bill repairs to an aluminium saucepan cost sixpence (2½p)!

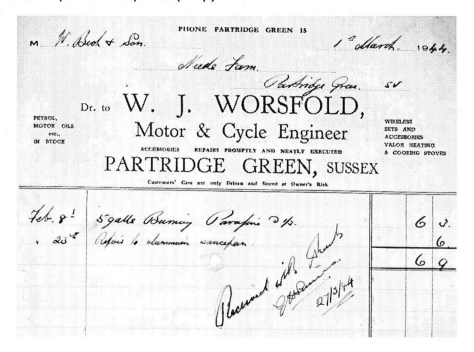

The Workers

All three of the Becks (William, Martha and son Louis) worked on the farm along with several members of another well known local family the Monnerys.

In June 1944 the weekly payroll was made up as follows:

George Stenning	Cowman, earning	£4 3s 3d	
Walter Monnery	Carter, earning	£3 16s 9d	
William Monnery	Stockman, earning	£3 16s 9d	
Frederick Monnery	Cowman, earning	£4 5s 9d	
George Hoadley	General, earning	£3 17s 9d	All had regular overtime payments.

Other help came in the form of seasonal labour for example; 'Golds, Hoeing mangolds £10', 'Boy, harvesting 10 shillings', 'M Gasson, Tractor work 7 shillings' and 'Thresher, 12 shillings'.

It's thought land girls were also used and a note in an undated jotter suggests prisoners of war from the nearby camps at Billingshurst and Thakeham were also put to use; '30 Dec two prisoners 5 hours each, 6 Jan two prisoners 2½ hours each'

The Workers climbing Needs Hill with the railway bridge in the background.

During World War Two

Talking to Fred Monnery it seems things didn't really change all that much just because of the war. Things were already changing with the introduction of tractors and other machinery such as balers and threshers and soon the combine harvester, along with advances in the milking parlour.

Fred Monnery at Needs Farm, putting a cluster on an udder in the automated milking shed which had been installed in 1936.

One thing he does remember is the black out curtains in the milking parlour, with milking starting in the dark hours every day it of course makes sense that the windows would need to be blacked out – but was the Fire Warden really that keen to be out checking at 5am?   Whether or not, those were the rules and if they hadn't blacked out the windows the lights could've been seen in Dial Post, so the windows were blacked out.

The farm, being bisected by the railway, was slightly at risk from enemy fire, indeed there were bullet holes in the cowshed roof, possibly resulting from the attack described by Cecil Longhurst: "We were putting a new roof on the granary at Clothalls and we saw this plane, well, there were always planes in the air. We took no notice of this one, we thought it was a Spitfire, but it was very low, treetop level and we saw the iron crosses under the wings. It machine gunned at us, carried on up the river firing at the prisoners cutting bushes on the river and on up the railway line. The people up at the Windmill Camp must have seen it 'cause they used their gun to try and bring it down. The plane started shooting at Henfield Station and carried on up the line, firing at us along the way. In those days there was a train, would come along and pick up the empty goods wagons, the train would quite often be as long as from here to Lock, all empty, but he fired at the train; only one bullet went through the driver's cab, but it killed the driver, all that gunning but he only killed one person."

Fred tells another tale about taking cover one day whilst out working in the fields at Griffins in Park Lane, when they heard the siren and ran for cover in a brick tunnel not far from the farmhouse. It was a hot summer day, very sticky and uncomfortable. On his way to take cover Fred had dropped his long awaited chocolate bar, by the time the all clear had sounded the bar had melted into a very gooey mess, not what Fred was looking forward to!

The tunnel where Fred and fellow workers hid in one air raid.

Talking of planes, below is an order to remove one of our own aircraft which came down on the farm in 1941. Nothing remains of the aircraft on the farm now.

R.A.F. Aircraft Collection Order

14/2/41.   Afternoon.

Description :-	Beau Fighter R. 2120.
Reference :-	
Serial No :-	47.
Category :-	E.
Location :-	North of Needs Farm, E. Grinstead.
Disposal Instructions :-	This aircraft has crashed into a wood and will require a tractor for salvage. The engines are partly buried and the whole machine is completely wrecked and scattered over the country-side. Collect and forward into Faygate for onward transmission.
Landowner :-	Mr. Peck, Needs Farm, PartridgeGreen.

45

Barrage Balloons were tethered here and there, we believe to protect the railway, it was hoped enemy planes wouldn't be able to get below the balloons to shoot the trains. There are still some remnants of the wire stays (pictured below, and now stapled to a fence post to avoid it getting caught in a hedgecutter) used to hold the balloons to the ground in some of the hedgerows along the public footpath from Well Land Farm to the disused railway line.

Another remainder from the war still visible in one or two places today where it reaches the surface, is a **communication cable** (pictured below) buried under the ground. We know very little about this either, but remains of it can be seen in the western gateway where the bridleway from Sextons Farm crosses the disused railway bridleway. It resurfaces in the pond half way across the field towards Hatterell Wood and again later to the north still on the Partridge Green side of the river by a stile over a stream. It is possible that it was only laid for exercise for the troops billeted in West Grinstead Park, and it may have only been used once or twice, but any other information about this would be gratefully received.

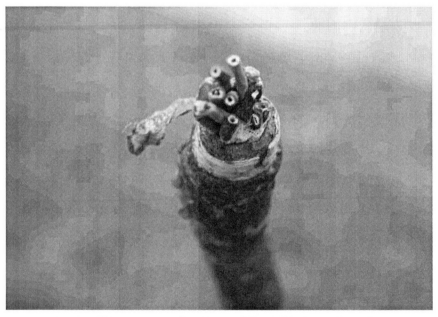

Part of the communication cable at Sextons Crossing
(approximately life size)

46

I guess one of the advantages of being on the farm during the war was the accessibility of food. Milk in particular providing the basis of most rationed food such as butter and cheese. Martha Beck would use the cows milk to make all the butter and cheese the farm needed and of course chickens were also in abundance, their eggs being collected and most sent off in boxes of 12 dozen down to Partridge Green station for onward transportation (usually Steyning Market), until the egg packing station opened in what is now the Huffwood Trading Estate. Then there were the animals themselves: cows, chickens and pigs — never any sheep at Needs though.

One of the boxes used to transport 12 dozen eggs at a time

Movement around the countryside was restricted, you only went to places if you had good cause to. One tale told by Louis is when he went to a market either to buy or sell something. He'd got his sister staying and she had decided to come along for the ride. They were stopped and questioned and I don't know if 'goods' were exchanged to secure their passage, but she didn't go for any more 'rides'.

Farming was a reserved occupation and although the Beck family men would have been too old to be called up to fight they were still able to contribute to the 'war effort' by farming the land they tenanted to its best advantage. Louis volunteered to join the ARP as a fire warden but was told he had enough hayricks and the like to be warden over without worrying about anything else and so was turned down. It seems he did quite a good job of worrying about his own farm as a Ministry report on the farm dated 17 April 1944 shows the farm to be working well, giving it an A grade. Farms slipping to C grades could be 'confiscated' by the Government and literally given to other farmers considered capable of making improvements.

Fred though was a member of the Partridge Green Home Guard, and like others I've spoken to found it quite demanding on top of a day's work. He'd finish up milking at quarter to eight in the evening, nip home for a bit of supper then off down the village at Partridge Green for 9pm Home Guard session. This could involve just keeping a look out, or undertaking an exercise or two, nothing too strenuous you'd think, but you try staying awake all night with nothing much going on and knowing you were going to knock off about 5 in the morning only to head straight to work to start the milking again! Ok, so Home Guard duty wasn't every day, but it meant at least once a week with no shut eye.

After the War

I'm not saying that the War didn't affect the farm, it of course affected everything, but the things that changed farming were not specifically war related. Mechanisation, as with every industry, changed farming. Horses which needed feeding, watering, shoeing, grooming etc every day were left by the wayside and forgotten along with the men who tended them. The tractors which could be left in the shed for weeks on end without attention and only needed fuel to do their work took over.

The combine harvester took the work away from the men who previously had to hand stack sheaves onto the wagon which carted the straw to the barn and then unload the sheaves to be threshed, then reload the straw to be carted to wherever it was to be stored and then of course unload and store it when it got there.

Two of the farm's horses, made redundant after the war

The cows were already being milked by machine, but of course the machine became more and more efficient and the cattle handling systems more proficient, making it only necessary for the one man to 'supervise' the same amount of cows. None of this happened quickly, the wage book for 1950 still showed all of the men who worked for the farm in 1944 apart from George Hoadley. But, instead of there being less men, two more had been taken on; Ernie Martin and M Oldroyd.

Today things have 'progressed' even further and less and less people work in agriculture at all. W Beck & Son in fact have no employees at all now and haven't done for about five years.

Diary of a 100-hour Week

By A V Sellwood (writing in July 1947 for the Sunday Graphic)

Farmer Beck works 112 hours a week. Cowhand Fred Monnery does nearly a hundred. And when they are "resting" both find time to tend well-stocked gardens. If you said to the farmer "You've a hard life" he wouldn't believe you. If you asked Fred Monnery why he gets up at 5am and cycles home from work at ten at night he would say "It's just my job". And it's going to be pretty tough for Britain if ever the thousands of Becks and hundreds of thousands of Monnerys decide to lead easier lives.

Today your milk ration has been cut by half a pint a week. Tomorrow? Well, Mr Beck and Mr Monnery are trying to fight that out for you right now.

Cameraman Wild and I arrived at Needs Farm, Partridge Green (Sussex) at 10pm. We found Farmer Beck and Fred Monnery side by side, shirt-sleeves rolled up, pitchforks in hand, perched on the top of a haywain. They were busy stacking hay on to an elevator that carried it to the top of a thirty-foot rick. They cleared one ton in eight minutes — which is *NOT bad going!*

Farmer Beck has a herd of a hundred Shorthorns, and 44 of them are producing 850 gallons of milk a week — the week's milk ration for nearly 3,000 people. Dairy farming sounds quite pleasant — easy, until you notice the lines beneath the suntan of the men who farm.

And for Farmer Beck the worst of the day was beginning. We went with him to his study. He lifted the top of his desk. "Silly Sussex they call us," he said. "Reckon we must be silly working like that and then coming back to this — still, it's the job". Inside the desk was a pile of papers, of cards, of forms in drab colours. Farmer Beck, on a Friday, must devote half an hour to working out just how much tax Whitehall wants deducted from the pay-sheets of the men who serve him.

Fred and Doris Elsie, the girl he married two years ago, were a little worried about the garden. "Don't seem to get much time to look after it," said Fred. "But it may be a hard winter—"

The description "Cow Hand" means
(a)   That he is able to drive and milk cows
(b)   Gather hay
(c)   Drive a tractor
(d)   Repair an automatic loader machine
(e)   Hoe out a field of kale and swedes
(f)   Handle a mower, clean out drains, sterilise milk churns, use a pitchfork.
And generally do a thousand and one things of which I haven't the foggiest idea.

This is the Day of the Farmer and Fred:
5am: Fred bikes a mile from his cottage to the milking shed. Farmer Beck walks from the homestead, helps drive the cows in.
5.30: Fred milks the cows. Farmer Beck supervises, schemes out the day's work etc.
8am: Breakfast. The sheds have been cleaned, cows milked.
9am: Fred sterilises the milk churns, drives a tractor to the hayfield. He helps load hay for cows on to the wains until midday.
1pm: Hay-loading, stacking it (when damp) in the barn; when dry on the fodder rick. Fred changes his job for a while to assist in the second milking.
5pm: Half-hour break for tea. Then the work goes on until 10pm. Often Farmer Beck — "I work seven days a week and am happy to do it" — is busy for another half hour or so.

Slogan of the Becks: "Make hay when the sun shines, but when it doesn't — well, there are lots of other jobs to do. Hoeing, clearing weeds, or when the ground is too "sticky", clearing out the sheds and farm buildings."

Trade and Commerce

By Dorothy Banks

Knepp Castle Blacksmith

In the 1930s there were three main centres of activity – West Grinstead, clustered around the station, Partridge Green and Dial Post, with a total population of less than 1,600[1]. Each had its own Post Office and shops, some more than others, and there were five pubs. In addition, lying between West Grinstead and Dial Post, was the Burrell Arms. This stood at the junction of the old A24 and the B2135; the fourth Post Office of the parish, incorporating a general store, was also there, along with a garage and a café. Nearby was a blacksmiths, serving the Knepp Estate, which is the only building to survive the dualling of the A24.

The Burrell Arms, run by Bill and Rosie Moulden, also acted as doctor's surgery on Tuesdays and Fridays. Rosie Moulden, described as a typical country woman with a heart of gold was quite a character, as Claire Walton's memoirs suggest, and lunchtime on these surgery days was an entertainment not to be missed:

"No-one who heard the conversational exchange at the Burrell Arms during Dr Matthews' lunch break would ever forget it. The meal had to be taken when Mrs Moulden had his food ready, and <u>not</u> when he was ready for it, so it was usually a rushed job, as most of the time he had patients waiting. Whilst the doctor ate she insisted on reading him what she considered were the day's vital news reports from the "Daily Telegraph". His consulting room was in the small back parlour and she read from the kitchen behind the bar, but this distance did not matter: she had a very loud strident voice and every sentence seemed to end in a screech.

The Burrell Arms

She soon had a larger audience when the bar was packed with those Canadian troops who could make it to witness this exchange. I am quite sure that this 15-20 minutes' performance every Tuesday and Friday lunchtime settled for ever any doubts they had ever had that the English were mad. The readings were frequently interrupted whilst Mrs Moulden added her own comments and even more frequently by questions such as "What do you think of that, Doctor?" Answers and suggestions from the bar were often not repeatable; from the belaboured doctor came usually a grunt or a rare 'yes' or 'no'. Once all the patients had been seen, Dr Matthews was at last allowed to glance at the paper himself when he had his cup of coffee in peace".

Of the four post offices in the parish, only the ones at the Burrell Arms and in Partridge Green could deal with telegrams and had sorting offices. In 1941 Lena Campbell and her sister Daisy Boniface took over the Burrell Arms Post Office and shop. In those days there was quite a community in that part of the Parish, and with the war effort in full swing the office was particularly busy with

---

1. 1931 census. There was no census in 1941.

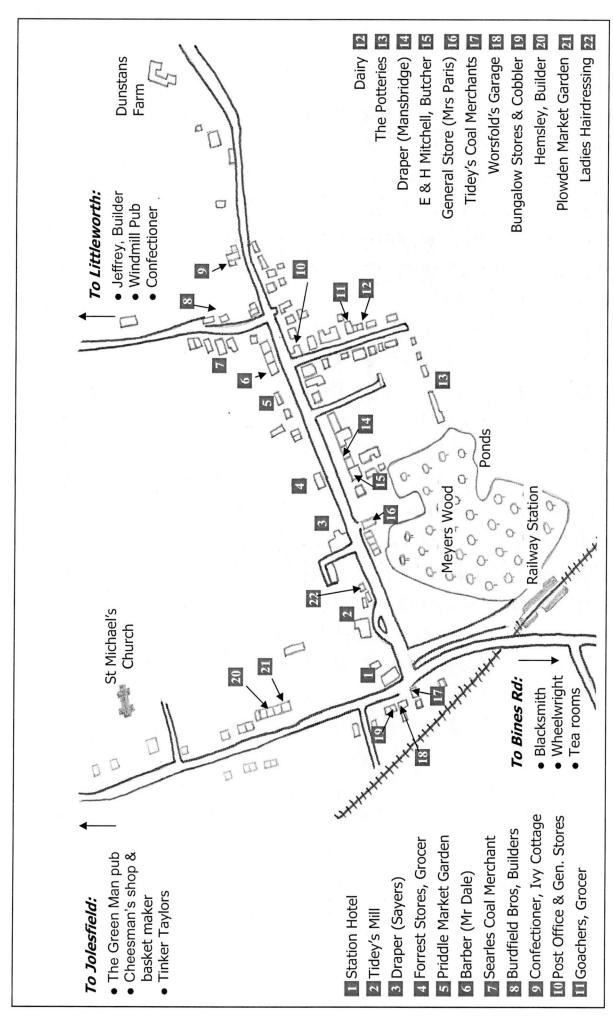

Shops and businesses in Partridge Green in the 1940s

To Jolesfield:
- The Green Man pub
- Cheesman's shop & basket maker
- Tinker Taylors

To Littleworth:
- Jeffrey, Builder
- Windmill Pub
- Confectioner

To Bines Rd:
- Blacksmith
- Wheelwright
- Tea rooms

1 Station Hotel
2 Tidey's Mill
3 Draper (Sayers)
4 Forrest Stores, Grocer
5 Priddle Market Garden
6 Barber (Mr Dale)
7 Searles Coal Merchant
8 Burdfield Bros, Builders
9 Confectioner, Ivy Cottage
10 Post Office & Gen. Stores
11 Goachers, Grocer
12 Dairy
13 The Potteries
14 Draper (Mansbridge)
15 E & H Mitchell, Butcher
16 General Store (Mrs Paris)
17 Tidey's Coal Merchants
18 Worsfold's Garage
19 Bungalow Stores & Cobbler
20 Hemsley, Builder
21 Plowden Market Garden
22 Ladies Hairdressing

St Michael's Church

Dunstans Farm

Meyers Wood

Ponds

Railway Station

telegram traffic for the Canadian soldiers quartered in Park House and Knepp Castle, as well as the traffic for West Grinstead Lodge, where many of Montgomery's staff were quartered prior to the D-day landings[1]. The schoolboy Douglas Martin, who lived at Wharf Cottages, helped deliver telegrams – alerted to his task by a flag put out for him; other helpers were Joan Brown from Southwater and, later, Evelyn May from Park Farm[2]. There were two deliveries by postal van from Horsham every day, and mail was dispatched three times a day – once by rail and twice by the Horsham van.

Partridge Green High Street with the Station Hotel in the foreground. Note the stripes painted onto lampposts and the kerb to help drivers in the black out.

At the start of the war, Partridge Green and Littleworth, which then consisted of about 150 houses, were positively awash with retailers and businesses compared with now – we have identified over 30 in this area alone, with the help of contemporary directories and the local knowledge of Doug Pennifold, Ginger Gee, Bob Dubbins and Mr King.

A visitor to Partridge Green might have alighted at the railway station on his way to a room at the Station Hotel (now the Partridge pub). In the goods yard there may have been men bagging coal – there were two coal merchants in the village: Dick Searles who had premises in Littleworth Lane, and Bob Tidey, who operated out of The Gables, next to Worsfold's garage (now Pretty's). As well as the Station Hotel, there were pubs in Jolesfield (the Green Man) and in Littleworth (the Windmill).

On Bines road was the blacksmith and farrier (now The Forge) owned by Mrs Gumbrill. Bill Pennifold, the wheelwright, "a craftsmen if ever there was"[3] worked at the back of the forge, in the building now known as the Smithy. At the Sheiling there was a teashop.

Heading north again, next to Worsfold's garage was what was known as the Bungalow Stores, where you could get sweets, tobacco and general goods, run by Mr and Mrs Jackson. Charlie Jackson was a cobbler, a skill very much in demand as shoes were rationed in the war, and he

---

1. Andrew Campbell   2. Claire Walton   3. Ginger Gee

could be found working long hours in his shed behind the shop.

There were four other similar shops: a lock up store at Ivy Cottage on the High Street; one in Littleworth, run by Mrs Browning, a confectioners and general store run by Mrs Cheesman at Jolesfield Common, and Mrs Paris' shop on the High Street next to New Cottages, which also sold newspapers. Mrs Paris was one day honoured by the confident arrival in her shop of Doug Pennifold, proudly equipped with his new sweet ration book, but unprepared for the possibility that he should also have to pay. Mrs Paris ran the shop by herself; Mr Paris being afflicted with asthma and chest problems, possibly as a result of years working as a brickmaker. Doug Pennifold remembers seeing "Mr Paris making bricks in Mr Allfrey's brickyard (which stopped operating in about 1934), which was south of Station Wood, where part of Star Trading Estate now is. The bricks were hand made, the clay being dug out by hand and brought to him in a wheelbarrow. His 'workshop' was no more than a corrugated iron roof structure and open to the weather on all sides. I can see him now with a hessian sack across his shoulders to keep off the rain".

In Church Road, still heading north, was Jack Hemsley the builder, who later became a manager on the Knepp Estate. Jack Hemsley, along with many others, was a regular at the Station Hotel on a Sunday. The story goes that he used to explain this to his children "by saying that when he came out of his house, he would roll a penny down his drive; if it turned up the road he would go to church, but if it turned left down the hill he would go to the pub." There were two other builders: Bill Jeffrey of Fern Hill, and Jack and Bert Burdfield in Littleworth Lane. Universally known as Ducky, Albert Burdfield also ran the school lorry and was organist and choir master at St Michael's after Mr Garton left in 1941. The Burdfields also ran an undertaking business from a field in what is now Hunters Mead.

The Hemsley business shared an entrance with Hugh Plowden's market garden which had a sales kiosk close to the road. The other market garden was on the High Street, next to Lynwood, and run by Mr and Mrs Priddle.

Behind Mrs Cheesman's shop at the entrance to the recreation ground on Jolesfield Common, Mr Julian Cheesman made baskets of every kind, despite being blind. The Cheesman's place was in the corner of the field owned by Partridge Green's rag and bone men, known by all as Tinker Taylors.

Mr and Mrs Priddle outside the greenhouse of their market garden at Nortonville, Partridge Green High Street

There are many tales regarding the Taylor brothers. Bob Dubbins recalls passing their yard on the way to school in the 1930s: "Tinker Taylors was a massive junk yard. It also housed besides the two occupants Mr Tom and Mr Steve Taylor an assortment of dogs — five in all — and a herd of nanny goats plus one billy goat who was not above giving chase if he felt that way when you met him in the neck behind Taylor's yard. The fact that there was a footpath through the neck made little difference as owners of land had little respect for footpaths in those days. You could walk them, but what happened whilst walking was your affair. So, if you had a rabbit skin for example, you gave the Taylors a shout which would be answered by a mad rush of barking, snarling hounds, followed, it was hoped (as it nearly always was) by Mr Tom. He was much the more civil of the two — always putting a 'Mr' in front of your name, no matter what your age. He would take the rabbit skin, inspect it, make some remarks about it being marked, or it was small, then sliding his hand in his breeches pocket right up to his elbow, produce a penny, or three halfpence.

"These two gentlemen were both soldiers in the 1914-18 War; both, I understand, unfortunately — as were so many of the brave young men of the period — were just put in the trenches as gun fodder and both got wounded — Steve to his stomach and Tom had a massive dent in his face.

"Their main mode of transport was by hand cart which Tom pushed around collecting smaller items. For the bigger items they had a Model T Ford lorry which, looking back on it now, was a bit of a laugh, if you could see it on take-off. Steve was the driver and he would get the Ford out, then out would come Tom with the dogs all roped together with a good strong cord. Right.... Tom is in the back behind the cab with the dogs in the cab. Tom, as well as being a passenger at the back is the look out. Before the off Tom looks behind and when the road is absolutely clear he gives a good sharp rap on the cab and off they go, usually with the dogs in full cry. It is also Tom's duty if anything is going to overtake, and also on slowing down to pull in to park, to give Steve a sharp rap on the cab if it's OK."

The lorry (in its various incarnations) and the brothers' driving exploits became something of a legend: Mr King remembers that they had an old lorry which they drove at about 10 miles an hour, carrying a milk churn of water in the back as the radiator leaked so badly that they had to stop every two or three miles to top up from the churn. Another tale, perhaps a variation, relates that "after years of driving the old lorry around, they were finally put off the road by the police, so Tom and Steve set about finding a replacement. They bought one from some way away and drove it home. In fact they went straight to Worsfold's garage because it had overheated and was boiling. The remedy was to give Steve and Tom some lessons on changing gear as it appeared they had driven some twenty miles in first gear".[1]

Most retail activity, however, was centred around the High Street in Partridge Green. There was a grocer in South Street at no 17, known as Goachers, and a larger Forrest Stores, run by Mr Lawrence, on the High Street where the Co-op now is. Baking was carried out at the rear of this store.

A third grocers was run by Mr Fisher at the Post Office (post mistress Mrs Ada Fisher) on the corner of South Street and the High Street. In addition to the telegraph, which had to be manned 24 hours a day in the war, this office also had a telephone exchange, manned by Melody Dayrell from 1944 (see photo overleaf). The exchange had some 190 numbers, covering Shermanbury, West Grinstead, Dial Post and Ashurst; the first premises to have telephone numbers were the public kiosk outside the Post Office, Tidey's Coal Merchants at the Gables, Tidey's Mill and Medway House at Jolesfield. The first stage of automation took place in 1948/9 and entailed moving the exchange to a new building behind "Leeacre" in the High Street and meant that all lines changed to consist of 3 numbers. (See also Appendix 1)

Mrs Ada Fisher of Partridge Green Post Office. Courtesy of John Fisher

1 Doug Pennifold

Just down the road from Goachers in South Street Nim Burdfield (cousin of Ducky) ran a milk delivery business from no 23 (Gresham). Nim delivered to outlying customers in a van, whilst the village was served by a cycle delivery. Doug Pennifold remembers working there in the holidays: "At the time, bottles were scarce and my instructions were only to deliver in exchange for an empty. Starting out on the bike with only a dozen or so bottles, it was a matter of continually returning to the 'depot' to wash the empties, refill them and fit them with a cardboard stopper (the middle of which could be pushed in to form a hole to pour from) before setting off again to continue the round. The washing facilities consisted of a bowl on an old table under the apple tree, often filled with only luke warm water; no rinsing or drying before refilling with a ladle from the churn."

At Fern Cottage in South Street was Alfred Castledine, listed in a local directory as an animals' dispenser. He acted as the unofficial vet, and it was to him that many a pet made its last journey.

At the bottom of South Street (which terminated then at a five-bar gate where Hazelwood Road now begins) lay The Potteries. Although nine brick or clay works have been identified as having existed at some time in West Grinstead parish, this is thought to be the only one still

Melody Dayrell, who worked at the manual telephone exchange at Partridge Green from about 1944, after leaving Jolesfield School, where she had won an award for fund raising for the War Effort.

operating by the beginning of the war, the brickworks at Partridge Green station having closed in about 1934. Operations had also ceased at the brick field next to Lloytscroft Cottages, although Roy Gasson remembers stacks of abandoned bricks there for years after the war. At the Potteries they made clay jugs, land drains, flower pots and all types and shapes of clay roofing tiles. The clay for making these was prepared in a mixer which was attached to an old cart horse which would walk round and round, mixing for hours on end.[1]

Back on the High Street, where the Hawthorn veterinary practice now is, was Mansbridge the drapers. A second outfitters was housed in Oak House, run by Mr and Mrs Basil Sayers.

The butchers, still there now, was run by Herbert Mitchell (his father Walter, "Old Mr Mitchell" as he was generally known, having retired to Wilton Villa), with Ernie Merritt (also Clerk to the parish council) an integral part of the team. On site was a slaughter house, with pig sties and chicken sheds behind. The butchery business had been operating since 1884, and remained in Mitchell hands for 105 years.

Finally, on our tour round the block, we come to Tidey's Mill. Owned by Jack Tidey it was a steam mill and corn merchants, selling animal feed, hay, straw etc. It became an egg packing plant soon after the war.

Dial Post was a small hamlet, which nevertheless had a school, a pub (the Crown) and a Post Office/grocers at what is now Pengates. There was also a guest house, Harry Grover's petrol filling station and Blakers welding business, which specialised in repairs to chassis and automotive parts.

---

1. Ginger Gee

There was another garage at Buck Barn, but most commercial activity in West Grinstead was close to the railway station. The Post Office and general stores was run by Stephen Tidey on the south of the road, and opposite lay the Tabby Cat Inn, licensee Mr Pankhurst.

The Tabby Cat at West Grinstead, looking east over the railway bridge

During the 1930s most retailers offered a regular, if not daily delivery service, and many households would have been able to avail themselves of the visiting salesman. For example, we know from Doug Pennifold that companies from Cowfold and Steyning delivered two or three times a week, fresh fish came from Stanley's of Shoreham and Funnells of Steyning and hardware from Haffendens or Scott and Sargent in Horsham. It was possible to get one's hair cut at Dennis Dale's in Orchard Cottage, Partridge Green High Street, a service also offered by Jess Merritt at Elm House or George Fairs in the Railway Cottages. The décor at Dennis Dale's "salon" was rather different from what one would expect today. He had a large plot of land down to orchard and vegetables, so according to the season there might be a pheasant hanging up to ripen, strings of onions, sacks of potatoes or boxes of apples stacked in the corner. Ladies could be looked after by a visiting professional hairdresser at Morningside. Clocks and watches could be repaired by Mr Turner in Short Row.

Given the restrictions caused by petrol rationing (or its total lack), general shortages and the effect of some 200 people being called up, it is unlikely that all these businesses and services survived the war unchanged. Perhaps it is more revealing to note which of them survive today in a recognisable form. Of the five pubs, four survive (the Tabby Cat as was is now a restaurant). One post office remains; we retain two of the three garages, one of the four grocers, the butchers at Partridge Green and Blakers in Dial Post.

Doctors and Nurses

By Julie Beck

There was no National Health Service during the war, but the parish then was served as it is now by the doctors at Henfield and Cowfold, but in addition there was a district nurse who lived locally.

Doctors included Dr Squires (father, son and grandson) and Dr Dickins amongst others. The nurse at the beginning of the war was Nurse Holden and she lived in the nurses bungalow near the old Jolesfield School. She was followed by Nurse Kiff towards the end of 1939.

Parishioners paid into a fund to pay for the nurse's services as the following extract from a March 1942 parish magazine explains:

District Nursing Association. – The Committee wish to bring to the notice of the parishioners the very real need there is for increasing our income. Various sums have been collected in the parish by Whist Drives, Dances and Entertainments. The sum of £30 was raised in October by a Jumble Sale in West Grinstead. But these efforts have not been sufficient to meet the increased expenditure. After careful thought it has been decided to alter the scale of charges for Benefit Subscribers as follows –

4s.	**4d.**	where the husband is serving in the Forces.
6s.	**6d.**	flat rate charge for all other families.
10s.	**0d.**	for Farmers and Tradesmen, as in previous years.

Subscriptions must be paid at the beginning of the Financial Year, e.g., April. Voluntary collectors will be glad to call as usual for the subscriptions. It should be noted that for those who do not subscribe, a payment of 1s. 3d. is charged for each visit Nurse is called in to make. It is therefore a good investment to become a Benefit Subscriber, as this enables the patient to have the necessary nursing care without further charges. Donations and voluntary subscriptions will be most welcome, and all efforts to raise funds for this most worthy cause will be much appreciated.

Below are the accounts for 1940 showing the subscriptions received and the expenses incurred by the nurse in her duties:

WEST GRINSTEAD DISTRICT NURSING ASSOCIATION
Statement of Receipts and Payments for Year ending 31st March, 1940

RECEIPTS	£	s.	d.	PAYMENTS	£	s.	d.
1. Voluntary Subscriptions	55	14	0	Nurses : -			
2. Benefit Subscriptions	61	4	10	1. Salaries (including Uniform allowance, &c.)			
3. Donations	15	16	2	a) Permanent Nurses	255	12	11
4. Proceeds of Entertainments, &c.	81	5	8	2. Pensions: County Pensions Scheme	27	0	0
5. Fees : -				3. Insurances	10	14	5
Midwifery	14	0	0	4. Housing Accomodation : -			
General Sick Nursing	4	6	8	a) Rent, Rates, Taxes	59	6	2
6. Grants per W.S.C.N.A. : -				b) Insurance (Fire, &c.)		5	0
a) From County Council for				5. Provision or Renewal of Nursing Equipment	1	2	6
Public Health Work	112	10	0	6. Transport Expenses	32	18	2
b) Ditto, for Nurses' Pensions	10	10	0	7. Administration : -			
c) Ditto, for Maintenance of Cars	25	0	0	Affiliation Fees	3	12	0
d) Ditto, for Telephone Rents	6	0	0	8. Printing and Stationery	1	13	10
e) Ditto, for General Nursing	2	0	0	9. Postage, &c.	7	11	0
7. Grant from Council for Measles and				10. Sundries : Cheque Books		10	0
Pneumonia Nursing Service	5	0	0	Steyning Nursing Association :			
8. Other Grants:				Repayment of half Ashurst Subscriptions	11	1	8
W.S.C.N.A. County Pensions Scheme	3	15	0	11. Balance in hand	45	7	0
9. Payment by Nurse towards Pension	9	0	0				
Ditto, for National Health Insurance	2	5	6				
10. Mileage Allowance, W.S.C.C.		18	2				
11. Sundries : Repayment of Rent on							
Telephone, 23rd September to							
31st December, and sundry calls	1	3	11				
Balance from previous year	46	4	9				
	£456	14	8		£456	14	8

Audited and found correct - (Signed) E. W. MERRITT, 17th April 1940.

Local resident Peggy Bennett who became a nurse herself wrote some time ago about medical treatment in the parish when she was young:

Peggy Bennett

'The District Nurse/Midwife went on her rounds on a sit up and beg bicycle, a basket on the handle-bars and her black bag strapped to the carrier. One did not necessarily have to see a doctor first before calling on her services – it was quite common to go to the nurse or call her in for ones needs, and she always seemed to be available although many patients were visited on doctors orders of course. Most people belonged to the local nursing association and paid a weekly subscription according to their means – anything from 1 penny upwards. Those who were too poor to subscribe – and there were some – obviously received free treatment, the Nursing Association paying what was necessary to the Nurse. Hence the need for continuous fund raising. Nurse Holden's husband was the dispensing chemist at Henfield pharmacy, a very useful contact as he could bring medicines home each day, as and when needed. I remember him cycling to and from Henfield in the early days but I guess around 1930 or so he required a small car that must have been a great help to him but not much to his wife who continued to battle to work on her bicycle. They were both very welsh and Nurse Holden had a lovely singing voice. Today it is hard to imagine those dedicated women carrying out their vital roles in various communities without any of the advantages of 'mod cons' as we know them. Their responsibilities were many and varied and often exceeded those of a hospital ward sister, who had all the advantages of the then up to date medication and conditions to hand.

Medicines were left at the nearest Post Office to be collected by patients or their deputies. If a doctor was needed urgently one had either to go to the nearest PO for a telephone or a nearby home which had the phone – the alternative was to go to Cowfold or Henfield to fetch the doctor yourself.'

During the war the following notices appeared in parish magazines:

We are asked to request parishioners, desiring the services of the Parish Nurse, to send their messages in writing when such messages are taken by children. It is a good plan to put all messages in writing if they are left at a time when the Nurse is out. (May 1941)

The Second Annual Meeting of the District Nursing Association was held in Partridge Green on May 30th. There was a good attendance. Miss Collins, the County Superintendent, gave a talk on Nursing and its meaning in relation to the community. She answered many questions. The number of visits paid by Nurse during the year was 3715. There are 232 benefitting subscribers. The balance sheet, showing a credit balance, had already been published. (June 1945)

And specifically in July 1941:

Dial Post Main Dressing Station for Civilians. We have had an interesting set of Lectures in our Village Hall. They have been on the subject of First Aid, and have been well attended. We are attempting to equip our First Aid Post according to a schedule drawn up for this purpose. It sets a high standard and involves a certain expense. By Whist Drives, Jumble Sale, Dance and collections, we have now in hand £13 14s. The last Whist Drive brought in £2 2s. 2d.

Can anyone spare us one of the following?: a marble topped wash-hand stand, old sheeting, hot water bottles and covers, chairs, jugs and basins, pillows or cushions, mackintosh sheet, bedrest pails, kettles, Primus or Beatrice stove, oil drum, wheel chair. Mrs. Warnett will be glad to hear of any such offers, or they may be made to Mrs. Wood at the Rectory.

The money for buying a Motor Car for the Parish Nurse has come in very well, thanks to the kind help given from all parts of the parish and from many friends. We need still more, and we are already on the look-out for a suitable second-hand car.

A Dance arranged for the Nursing Association at Dial Post by Mrs Philpott, Mrs Field and Mrs Longhurst during the month brought in £8 10s, and a Whist Drive arranged by Mrs Philpott and helpers brought in £5 14s. Mr Fisher of Partridge Green has sent in £5 16s as the result of a Dance and a Whist Drive.   (June 1941)

Thanks to the generosity and good-will of many friends, the District Nurse now has a car for use in her work. Mrs. J. P. Hornung kindly took up the responsibility of initiating the fund for purchase. She received donations from many quarters in the parish. Various activities were set going in addition, resulting in the collecting of £62 16s. 11d., or nearly half the amount. The total sum collected was £143. This pays for the car, for the improvement of the garage, and for the first year's Insurance.

The following list gives the proceeds of parochial activities: In Partridge Green – Mrs. Gumbrell's Jumble Sale (half proceeds), £8 15s.; Mr. Fisher – Dance and Whist Drive, £6 8s. 6d.; another Dance, £1; a Draw, arranged by Miss Davis, with Mrs. Kidd, £18 14s.; Stoolball Dance, £3 14s.; Jolesfield House Garden Display, given by Jolesfield School, £3 15s. 2d. In Dial Post; the proceeds of a Dance and Whist Drive brought £16 6s. 4d. The four Post Offices put a collecting box on the counter. The total result of these boxes was £4 3s. 5d. The Committee of the Nursing Association thank sincerely all those who in any way helped towards the happy result.   (July 1941)

Home Guard Dressing Station, Dial Post. With the kind permission of the Officers and men of the Home Guard, in giving up their lecture room, the women of Dial Post have been able to fit up a Dressing Station for the civilians, as well as for the Home Guard, in the event of a blitz or an invasion. It has only been possible to do this with the help of the people in the surrounding district coming forward with their advice and contributions. There are lectures given every Wednesday evening by an Army Doctor, who has given excellent advice on the care of the wounded.

I am making an appeal for old sheets, towels, blankets, etc., of which we are in great need. If anyone has any of these articles, would they let Mrs. Wood at the Rectory, or Mrs. Warnett, Dial Post, have them, or they would be called for. Thank you. A. E. Warnett.   (July 1941)

Nurse Holden was well respected in the parish:

Nurse Holden has been Parish Nurse for twenty years. How many householders have an unforgettable experience of her love and care in time of trouble? What patience in the daily round! What heavy anxiety and quiet confidence when a patient is between life and death, and under God, the Nurse brings the patient back to health! Every parishioner who has known her bears testimony to her skill. She knows nearly every house in the parish and has known nearly all the inhabitants. She could tell many a story of the ten years in which, in all weathers, she did her work on a bicycle. She has seen many changes in the evolution of the parish nurse. At first, district nursing was supported by voluntary contributions. The State quickly saw what the nurse was capable of doing in a parish, and developed State services using the parish nurse, and making grants. An important part of the parish nurse's work is the regular supervision of the school children. We see the difference in the children's health and welfare.

Mr Holden, her husband, has taken over a business in Alton, Hants., known as the King's Library. This, then, is to be their address when they leave. Mr. Holden will be much missed for his own sake. He has a generous nature, with a wide and generous outlook on men and women. We hear very continuously of kindly services done by him in unseen ways. He and Nurse very frequently placed their car at the disposal of those who for reasons of trouble or poverty needed a lift to hospital.

At the Parish Church, Nurse has been leader of the Choir. Always in her place, except when other duties detained her, she was a real help in bringing us to keep good tunes and new tunes. She led in the anthems and often sang solo. Mr. Holden was sidesman, and could always be relied upon when anything was to be done. There is no doubt that both Mr. and Mrs. Holden will be very much missed. Our memories of them will be happy ones. Many will add to these memories those of deep gratitude for her personal service in time of need.   (August 1939)

To replace Nurse Holden came Nurse Kiff:

We are fortunate in having Nurse Kiff for our District Nurse. She is a Queen's Nurse. We have found it necessary to raise our fees for people who are not subscribers. The minimum fee will now be 1s. a visit. It is well to remember that the collectors will be asking for the annual subscriptions in April. The minimum subscription is 4s. 4d., or 1d. a week, and this for the free services of Nurse for any member of the family during the following twelve months. If every household in the parish would become a subscribing member, it would greatly benefit our financial position. We want all the financial help possible to keep this excellent and necessary work in our midst. (February 1941)

By the kindness of Mr. and Mrs. Kidd, a Fete was held in their beautiful garden on Aug. 5th. The proceeds were given to the District Nursing Association. A large number of friends in Partridge Green co-operated with the Committee. The result was a great success. The weather was beautiful. The crowd numbered between 300 and 400. The proceeds amounted to £111 12s. 6d. Many thanks to all concerned.

Cash Statement.

		£	s.	d.	£	s.	d.
Donations -							
Mrs. Binny		1	0	0			
Mrs. Doxat		1	0	0			
Miss Edgell			10	0			
Mrs. Harvey		2	0	0			
Mr. W. Morgan		1	0	0			
Mrs. Peacock			5	0			
Mr. and Mrs. Plowden		1	0	0			
Mr. Sidebottom		1	10	0			
Bishop Wood		1	0	0			
					9	5	0
Stalls –							
Jumble	a) Clothes, etc.	25	17	7			
	b) Household	7	18	3			
					33	15	10
Fancy Articles					13	4	8
Produce					5	1	3
Side-shows					23	8	1
"Draws"					15	9	10
Teas					2	16	0
Admissions					4	4	6
Whist Drive (per Mrs. Darrington)					1	8	0
Dance (per Mr. Fisher)					5	5	0
					113	19	0
Less –							
Burdfield Bros.		1	10	0			
Printing			7	6			
Buns			6	0			
Milk			3	0			
					2	6	6
					111	12	6

(September 1942)

There was also access to an ambulance service set up in Henfield in 1934. A new ambulance was acquired in October 1944, money being raised by subscription to buy it. Mr Frank N Clarke, the president of the Henfield and District Ambulance Club wrote a letter to the parish in 1943 answering queries as to the vehicle's use:

With regard to transport of patients, who are members of our Ambulance Club, from Hospital to their homes. If they are stretcher cases and certified as such by the medical man, the ambulance may be called upon. If not stretcher cases, but too ill to travel other than by car, they are then sent home by car, under what is known as the "Pool Scheme". This is arranged by the Hospital. I understand we have already had cases of this kind. Both are free of cost to the patient. I hope this gives you the information you require – if anything else, drop me a line.

Joy Gibson, née Mitchell, remembers when she was about five or six an accident in the butcher's shop which required medical attention:

'I was never allowed in the shop when my father was around, but when he went up to Horsham to get the allocated meat for the shop Uncle Ernest (Merritt), he was kind and let me go in the shop. On one of these occasions I'd hung all the hooks around the drawers and somehow put my leg on it and put a big hind quarter hook right through my leg, in one side and out the other. That was at the beginning of the war when Dunkirk was on, there was no hospital available. They took me over to Wilton Villa, my grandparents' house, laid me out on the big dining room table and operated on my leg.

Dr John Squires' father was doctor at Henfield, but he'd gone back into the air force and so his father had come to stand in for them and so it was Dr John Squires' grandfather that operated on my leg. They had to clean it all out, especially as it was a meat hook you see. Luckily it was slightly bent and it pushed the main artery to one side.

I woke up, back at home, and an aunt of mine who was a Red Cross Nurse came and looked after me. They kept me in bed for such a long time whilst it mended, that when I stood up my leg didn't reach the ground. They found a little tricycle for me to get about and stretch my leg. There was a big old pram and my brothers would have races in Partridge Green High Street with me in the pram.'

It's difficult to say whether medical services are improved these days; on the one hand medicine has advanced tremendously, but it seems community spirit and investment by local patrons helped take care of some of what we now take for granted, or without funding just doesn't happen at all.

The Parish Church During the War

By Julie Beck

It seems from people's recollections and the parish magazines for the time that services at St George's, St Michael's and in Dial Post (held in the school) continued in one way or another throughout hostilities.

The following extract from a parish magazine dated January 1939, before the war started shows the clergy, church wardens, sidesmen, parochial church council members amongst others, along with details of services.

WEST GRINSTEAD with PARTRIDGE GREEN.

Rector: The Right Rev. CECIL J. WOOD, D.D.

Churchwardens: Capt. George Hornung and Mr. A. F. Pacey.

Sidesmen.—West Grinstead: Messrs. Holden, Taylor, Short, Fred Philpott, Greenfield, Tom Barnett, Jesse Tidey, and Capt. Bell. **Partridge Green:** Messrs. Eldridge, Gumbrill, Voice, Kildahl, Hudson, Nim Burdfield, Eason, Jones, Darrington, Stephen Tidey.

Organists: Mr. N. Mitchell and Mr. P. Garton.

Parochial Church Council.—Messrs. A. L. Short, A. J. Medland, A. Garrard, Jesse Tidey, Mrs. I. M. Green, Mrs. A. J. Bell, Mrs. G. W. Verrall, Mrs. Newnham, Mrs. C. J. Wood, and the Church-wardens, Messrs. P. Garton, E. Gumbrill, J. Burdfield, B. Kildahl, G. Voice, Mrs. Thomson-Glover, Mrs. Gumbrill, Mrs. Garton, Miss D. Gosset, Miss G. B. M. Edgell, Mrs. Carr, Mrs. Eason, Mr. J. Hoadley, Rev. H. D. L. Viener.

Representatives to Diocesan Council: Mr. A. F. Pacey, Mrs. Gumbrill, Mrs. Viener.

Representatives to Ruri-decanal Council: Mr. A. F. Pacey, Mrs. Thomson-Glover, Miss D. Gosset.

The Nursing Association.—Collectors: Mrs. Warnett (for Dial Post); Mrs. H. Tidey (for Station, Kennels, westward to the Bar); Miss V. Gosset (for Partridge Green); and Miss M. Gaisford (for Littleworth).

Verger & Sexton at W.G.: Mr. Henry E. Harding. **Verger & Sexton at P.G.:** Mr. Henry Penfold.

CHURCH SERVICES.

West Grinstead. — Every Sunday : Morning Prayer at 11.30 a.m.; Evensong at 6 p.m. Holy Communion on 1st and 5th Sunday in month at 8 a.m.; on 2nd and 4th Sunday at 11.30 a.m. Sunday School at 10.30 a.m.

Partridge Green. — Every Sunday : Morning Prayer at 10.15 a.m.; Evensong at 7 p.m. Holy Communion on 2nd and 3rd Sunday at 8 a.m.; on 1st and 3rd Sunday at 10.15 a.m.

Dial Post.—On 4th Sunday in month, Holy Communion at 8.30 a.m. Sunday School as arranged. Friday, 7 p.m., Mission Service.

On Holy Days and Saints' Days: Services by announcement.

With the arrival of evacuees in Partridge Green, the services at St Michael's were adjusted:

In order to make the Sunday services as suitable as possible for all concerned we are making a change at Partridge Green. At 10.15 a.m. on Sunday mornings we are having a service for children specially. We want every child of school age to come. We shall pray together for father and mother who stay in London and for God to deliver us from our enemies. We shall ask that we may be brave and true. Also that God will guide our Prime Minister and the Government with the wisdom of the Holy Spirit. This service will begin on Sunday Oct 1st. We shall be very glad of some grown-up people to come and sit with the children and to help find their places. The service will be over by 10.55. It will begin punctually.

On and after Sunday, Oct 1st, morning service will be at 11 a.m. during the time that the evacuees are with us. I shall be interested to see how this suits people. The morning service at 10.15 a.m. has shown that it meets the convenience of many. If the 11 a.m. service proves to be less suitable, we shall return to the hour of 10.15.

Evensong on Sundays will be said in both churches at 3 p.m. The services of Holy Communion remain as at present. Until Mr Peacock is ordained to the Priesthood it is not easy to alter them. Take the opportunities that come in your part of the parish.

Looking through the parish magazines from before war and on past the end of the war, services were subject to change, sometimes at short notice. Precise reasons were not often given, presumably because of censorship, but mainly changes came about because of the lack of clergy and, in particular, evensong times changed in the winter to avoid blackout problems.

The church became more of a focal point especially for those with family and friends away from home, or indeed, for those being away from home themselves. Although the parish magazine was not distributed free of charge to all, it does seem to have been a very important means of communication for both churchgoers and those who weren't, whilst of course face to face contact at services also became a valuable means of communication and support.

The People

The Rector, Bishop Wood, had deferred retirement in order to hold the reins of the Parish during the hostilities, as unlike Revd F H Campion, the incumbent when World War 1 broke out, Bishop Wood was over the upper age limit to be called up, even to serve as a chaplain as Campion did.

Bishop Wood was inducted at St George's church in November 1933, on the eve of the anniversary of Armistice Day. He stayed through the war, apart from a short absence due to illness, eventually leaving in 1947. The parish magazine for July 1943 reports, 'Bishop Wood is away in a Nursing Home for some three or four weeks, and hopes to return towards the end of August. With the assistance of the Bishop of Chichester, he is doing his best to arrange for normal Sunday services. But with many Clergy away as War Chaplains, this is not easy. Notices will be put on the Church Door.' Bishop Wood and his wife lived in the house currently used as the Rectory at West Grinstead. Although they had a car, it's thought they only received the same petrol rations as everyone else, so most of their ministering was carried out by bicycle.

It may be of interest to know that the Bishop of Chichester was brother to both Mrs Wood and the lay reader Captain Bell, who lived at Midway House on Jolesfield Common, so it's possible that the parish may have had more support from Chichester than other parishes.

The following paragraphs about the Rector and one of the curates come from Claire Walton (née Campbell)'s memories about the war.

'Spiritually the parish was in the competent hands of the Rector – Bishop Cecil Wood – and his wife, who worked ceaselessly to help all parishioners whatever their needs as far as possible, and his curate Rev Colvin Lewis. The latter lodged in the house at the corner of the High Street and South Street, opposite the Post Office. Mr Lewis travelled round the village by bicycle, so did the Bishop and his wife for much of their ministry here. The Bishop intended to retire about the time hostilities started, when war was inevitable he and Mrs Wood – who was sister of Bishop Bell of Chichester – decided to stay on for the duration of war.

Sunday services were attended by the Bishop and Mr Lewis, although none could be held in the evenings during winter months because of the near impossibility of blacking out either church efficiently. So Sunday afternoons became the order of the day for Evensong, with that service held at Dial Post quite regularly in the school assembly hall at that time, later it was transferred to the village hall in the evenings – the black out no longer mattered after peace was declared.

Once we moved to the Post Office [by the Burrell Arms] Mr Lewis was a frequent visitor on a Sunday to tea or supper, as we were on his route home. We never knew definitely when he was coming, he would just appear on the doorstep and somehow there was always something to eat! He amused us all with tales of his childhood in S. Africa, where he was brought up early 1950. He kept up a correspondence with my mother and aunt until he died, some years later.

Bishop Wood had been Bishop of Melanesia in the South Pacific and Mrs Wood, a trained nurse had started a form of health and welfare service there, where nothing of that kind had ever been heard of before. She was marvellous during the war with her welfare work overseeing much of it with the help of members of the Mother's Union – keeping in touch with most of the servicemen and women of the parish. Her knowledge of conditions in the Far East, which both she and the Bishop know quite well, proved invaluable to those who were posted to that war zone. Once again, their car was not all the help it might have been to them, for they got no extra petrol for their parochial duties either and often had to fall back on the use of their trusty cycles.'

Other curates included:
Rev L V Peacock who came in March 1939 and left in March 1941, 'The Rev L V Peacock has been appointed to a Chaplaincy in the RAF and has taken up his duties. The Easter Offerings at St Michael's, Partridge Green, will be given to him in appreciation and gratitude.'

After six months of being vacant, the position of curate was filled by Rev Michael Townroe from Grantham Parish Church on Sunday 12th October 1941.   He lived for some of his time in the parish at Copyhold after Mrs Langton moved out to do 'war work'. Whilst in residence Rev Townroe met his wife, Beatrice MacDougall, and they were married on 10th October 1942 at the Chapel of the Community of St Hilda, at Micklepage. He also became Deputy Pastor and Leader of the Community.

He left in 1944, 'after three years ministry with us, [Rev Michael Townroe] will be leaving in October, to take up work at Pulborough. It should be a larger work in a larger parish. His many friends here will remember with gratitude his ministrations, and will thank God for the many things he has been able to do here. His connection with Micklepage kept him in touch with points of view which scarcely come into parish work, but which enrich the mind and indirectly bring inspiration into all his work.'

Money was donated towards repairing 'Bomb Damage' to St Michael's as a parting gift. A fund had been set up in September 1944 after the 'Parochial Church Council held a meeting at Partridge Green on Sept. 4th and received a report on the bomb damage to the church. The Council accepted the fact that a certain amount of money would need to be raised locally towards the repairs though the major part would be raised by the War Damage Commission.' An iron protection had been set against the east window to form protection against blast back in 1941 as apparently the window is 'valuable and good. Blast acts in ways which are variable. This may also be a protection against splinter and other missiles under a certain weight.'

Rev C H Cox took on the reigns from December 1944 until February 1945, a short stay seemingly down to being unable to find anywhere to live according to the January 1945 magazine; 'It is still uncertain whether the Rev C H Cox will be able to stay in Partridge Green. So far he has not been able to find a house.'

The position remained vacant again until Rev G H Colvin Lewis came in September 1945.

Other Changes

We've seen from Claire Walton's memories that winter evensong had to be brought forward into daylight hours because of the impracticalities of blacking out the church windows, which was also the case in neighbouring Henfield, there they even had to remove the shiny weathercock from the church tower.

Here, as it was across the whole country the church bells were silenced. Not least because of the lack of men, (women had also been ringing at St George's by this time), but also the proposal for the ringing of church bells to signify invasion.

According to a report sent to the bellringing journal 'The Ringing World' by Cecil Longhurst, the bells at St George's were only rung after the Battle of Alamein for Sunday service, and only then with members of other towers to make up the numbers. Although none of the band died during

World War 2 (unlike WW1), it seems their strength dwindled for some time after the war; records show numerous peals of 2 hours and more being rung in 1937, but not again until the 1950s.

A tale is told about services during the war years, that whilst enjoying a drink at the Burrell Arms you could be joined by certain members of the choir from St George's who would appear for a quick drink having nipped out during the Rector's sermon. It must have been some sermon, the pub being at least a five minute trot away over the fields. Another memory is that of an uninvited visitor to the pulpit. Whilst the congregation were sitting in their pews eagerly awaiting their sermon, a man all dressed in black came in. He had a black hat, black trousers and of course a black shirt. He ran up in to the pulpit and started shouting forth. His words were frowned upon and no-one ever spoke of the incident.

Sunday School appears to have run as normal during the war years under the guidance of Mrs Carr. Christmas parties and trips to various benefactors' gardens for tea were arranged along with the general tuition of the scriptures on a Sunday.

Part of the church's remit during the war was, as it is now, along with baptisms and funerals, a place for the joining of man and woman in holy matrimony, or if you like, marriage. One wedding that I know of which took place during hostilities was that of local girl Betty Gumbrill to Kenneth Howall Thompson on 14th September 1940. Betty, daughter of village blacksmiths Albert and Alice Gumbrill, lived at Guess Gardens on Bines Road. Betty's wedding was held at St George's and as you can see from the photograph of Betty coming into the church on her father's arm, the gravestones on the front lawn had yet to have been levelled at that time.

Betty Gumbrill with her father, Albert E Gumbrill, the village blacksmith and sidesman at Partridge Green (St Michael's), on her way into church for her wedding in 1940

Her dress, although not white, was clearly a special dress, falling to her ankles and with a pretty flower motif material. She didn't wear a veil or carry a bouquet, just wore a corsage of four carnations, which appear to match the gentlemen's buttonholes. Obtaining silk, let alone white silk wouldn't have been easy during the war. Both the bride and the groom are holding gloves, much more popular than nowadays. I don't suppose with the silencing of the church bells that the now traditional pulling off of the treble simultaneously with the bride and groom stepping out into the porch happened, so the happy couple missed out on the pealing of the bells celebrating their union.

Another wedding which took place during the war was that of Hornung descendant Miss Suzanne Du Boulay in 1941, reported as follows in the parish magazine. 'The Parish Church was full for the marriage of Miss Suzanne Du Boulay on Dec. 21st to Lord Douglas Gordon. Many had seen her grow up from childhood, and affectionately wished her god-speed in her new life. There was an augmented choir, part being from West Grinstead, part from Partridge Green, and the singing was well done. Two pipers of the Black Watch played them from the Church. The reception was held at Ivorys. The decorations of the Church were by Mrs. Courtauld. The wedding was picturesque and beautiful. The bridesmaid was Miss J. Swinnerton Dyer. The attendant children were Virginia Murray, Diane Du Boulay, Peter Du Boulay and Henry Green. They were most charming.'

At one time the number of people away from home serving their country was so great that not all could be prayed for by name in one service, as this extract from the March 1944 magazine reports:

Prayer for those in the Forces. – It has been suggested to me that during the next few critical months, it would be right and good to remember by name, at some time in our Church, all those serving in the Forces. As the list of those who have gone from this parish contains the names of over 200 men and women, it would not be possible to remember them all at one service. And so we shall adopt the plan of remembering so many by name at each of the two main services on Sunday, and then, as we have always done, remember them all in silence, followed by a prayer. (The letters refer to the surnames of the men and women who will be remembered especially at the services on the day mentioned).

> 1st **Sunday in the month.** – 10.30 a.m. All whose names begin with A and B.
> 6.30 p.m. All those whose names begin with C, D and E.
>
> 2nd **Sunday in the month.** – 10.30 a.m. All whose names begin with F, G and H.
> 6.30 p.m. All whose names begin with I, J, K and L.
>
> 3rd **Sunday in the month.** – 10.30 a.m. All whose names begin with M, N and O.
> 6.30 p.m. All whose names begin with P, Q and R.
>
> 4th **Sunday in the month.** – 10.30 a.m. All whose names begin with S, T and U.
> 6.30 p.m. All whose names begin with V, W and Y.

During the weeks and months that lie ahead we could not do better than to have in mind the words of Tennyson: "More things are wrought by prayer than this world dreams of." Our prayers for others, if prayed after the manner of Our Lord's prayer, and in and through Him, will help, strengthen and sustain them in more ways than we shall ever know about or fully realise. Many of those whom we love are so fully occupied that they have little time for quiet and prayer themselves, many are facing, or will be facing, great danger and hardship; all of them, at home, abroad or prisoners of war, we can surround with the love and power of God through our prayers. We can help each other, and help them best if we come together and pray for them together. Come and pray for those whom you know as friends, as well as for those who are near and dear to you. If you are prevented by any urgent reason from coming, you can join with us wherever you may be, for you will know from the above plan whom we are praying for at each service.

Michael Townroe.

The magazine for December 1946 talks about how the servicemen and women were welcomed back to the parish:

> The "Welcome Home" has been happily disposed of. Each section of the parish raised its own fund and took its own line. Dial Post held a Social and distributed the money as a token of "gratitude for war service in the Forces for the common cause." Each member welcomed received an envelope with £1 11s. 6d. in it.
>
> The Fund at Partridge Green has taken rather the same line. A Social is being held, with an Entertainment. Each member welcomed receives £1 7s. 6d., as a token of friendship and gratitude.
>
> At West Grinstead a Welcome Home Supper is being held, with an entertainment to follow. Nearly 100 sit down to the supper.

Earlier in July 1945, several Prisoners of War had returned and been welcomed back with a packet of bank notes:

PARISH NOTES

> A very happy evening was spent in Partridge Green Village Hall in giving a welcome to five returned Prisoners of War : Warrant-Officer Frank C. Wells, Gunner Albert Leslie Burton, Gunner Eric J. Chase, Private W. Peacock and Gunner Bert Tiley. After tea a parcel of Bank Notes was presented to each. There was little speech-making. The atmosphere was one of congratulation and thankfulness. A delightful entertainment was given by Mr. Jacobson and his troupe, from Lambeth. The evening was rounded off with a dance.
>
> At Dial Post, Driver Fred Philpott and Gunner Arthur Bradley were each greeted by their friends on returning from Prisoners of War Camps on the Continent. They came back at different times. But each was presented with a packet of Bank Notes in congratulations on their safe return.

Victory thanksgiving services were also held, and children's parties were held around the parish to celebrate the end of the war.

When nearly all of the troops had returned home two very different events were held as the parish magazine for January 1947 reports:

> The "Welcome Home" Supper at West Grinstead was a great success: over 70 guests sat down to it in West Grinstead Church Room. A hot supper was served by F. W. Mitchell Ltd., of Worthing. The toast of "The King" having been drunk, Lt-Col. Geo. Hornung proposed the toast of those who had served in the Forces. Among the speakers were Lt.-Col. Brian Adams, Major Henry Green, Miss Veronica Hornung, Mr. Bob Grosse, and Mr. Pallant. The company stood for a moment's silence in grateful remembrance of John Grantham and Fred Budd, who went from here and did not return. An hour's entertainment was provided by "The Versatile Pair" from Brighton. Mr. Pallant later played for community singing, and a very happy evening came to a close.

> The "Welcome Social" in Partridge Green Village Hall brought a full audience. The evening opened with a splendid entertainment from London professional variety entertainers, kindly brought to us by Mr. Rowe, who presided at the piano and gave musical sketches. A presentation of an envelope with a money gift inside was made to 88 returned members of the Forces. A few of these members are still abroad, and their gift is being sent to them. The names of the fallen were read, and all stood in silence with thoughts of remembrance, thanks, and sympathy with the bereaved. After the serving of refreshments there was a dance. The evening was organized and arranged by members of the Parish Council and was voted a great success.

War Memorials

By Julie Beck

There are three war memorials that I have looked into. They are to be found inside St George's church, outside St Michael's church and at the end of the drive to Needs Farm (opposite the end of Mill Lane), the latter pictured below.

1939 - 1945

F. BUDD	H.C.T.KNIGHT
H. FLINT	A.C. LUCAS
L. FINCH	G.W. MITCHELL
P. GANDER	W.B. SAYERS
J.R. GRANTHAM	D. WEAVER

Memorials in the graveyard at St George's

Hugh Verrall

Serial No.	6405435
Graveyard area 8	L/cpl H G W Verrall
Row 1	The Royal Sussex Regiment
Plot 16	14th October 1940
	Aged 45
	Soldier and Artist
	1914 -1918 & 1939 – 1940
	The lord gave and the lord taketh away.

Hugh's family lived and farmed at Hobshorts and Thistleworth during the second world war. He served in both wars, but died as a result of injuries sustained in a train accident in London.

He had exhibited in the Royal Academy between the wars, famed for paintings of agriculture and local farms, although his sketch pad went with him most places and contains many drawings of soldiers in action and at rest.

Hugh Verrall's War Grave

Although Hugh has a war grave in West Grinstead, he is not on any of the war memorials in the Parish.

Claude Mitchell   In proud and loving memory of Sub Lieut (A) Claude W Mitchell
Graveyard area 6   R N V R
Row 4   Who lost his life 30th May 1945
Plot 10   off the coast of East Africa from HMS Colossus
    Aged 20 years.

Brother to Geoff and Joy Mitchell. Son of Herbert, butcher in Partridge Green and Rose, a schoolteacher at Itchingfield. The parish magazines often reported Claude's memorable performances in youth club plays and shows.

Claude joined up after leaving Steyning Grammar school and became a commissioned officer and a navigator. He did his training in Trinidad and moved over towards the Red Sea Area with his ship HMS Colossus. He was lost at sea when his plane failed to return from a mission.

Inside St George's the WW2 memorial tablet lies below the larger tablet for WW1. Note the difference in the number of men killed in the two wars. Also inside the church is a bookcase dedicated to the memory of John Grantham, whose story is told on the following pages.

John Grantham

WAR MEMORIAL GIFT—Mr. and Mrs. Grantham have made a gift to the parish church in memory of their son who was killed while serving with the R.A.F. in the war. It is being made by Messrs. Fowler Bros. and will be a bookcase in wood to match the old wood in the church and to contain the new hymn books and prayer books which we are buying. The P.C.C. at their last meeting gratefully accepted this gift, and we hope it will be ready by May.

Extract from a Parish Magazine for April 1948.

Mrs Grantham's maiden name was Fowler, which explains the bookcase being made by Fowler Bros of Cowfold.

Di Holman, John's sister, who still lives in the parish and is a regular worshipper at St George's kindly took the time to tell me his story.

John and his sister and brother Tony were born in Cowfold and the whole family moved to Bowshotts Cottage in the early thirties. Di would bike to Cowfold for school from the family home next to West Grinstead station. John cycled to Jolesfield when he first went to school, and then when he was older he caught the train from home down the line to Steyning. The train went through the brooks south of Henfield which when flooded were like going across the sea. John is also commemorated on the school war memorial at Steyning Grammar.

*John top left with school friends, including Alan Jones sitting on the swing.
Photo taken circa 1935.*

John on his bike

72

Whilst still at school John, whose father's livelihood involved horses in every shape and form, was respected for his horsemanship, one notable ride being at the County Show at Eastbourne in 1939 which the following extract from a letter to his father describes, 'Well there was only one competitor worth watching, a slip of a boy from W Grinstead by name John Grantham." The reporter also described him as a 'little artist on a horse'.

The photographs show (left) the 14 year old 'little artist' receiving his prize from Lavinia, Duchess of Norfolk at the County Show, Eastbourne 1939 and (right) 'flying' on his horse at Loxwood.

He wasn't only an 'artist on a horse'. He is also rather famed for his capture of the railway train being machine-gunned in 1942 at West Grinstead Station, being adjacent to his home.

His drawing reproduced below shows a plane making its attack on the train, whose driver, George Ansbridge (from Horsham) was unfortunately killed.

Drawing by 17 year old John Grantham in 1942

Six months after this incident John qualified as 'Sgt Air Gunner'.

Having been a cadet in the Air Training Corps at Steyning he'd had the chance to try gliding and I suppose having enjoyed that immensely, and having decided to volunteer for service, the Air Force was a natural choice.

John served for 15 months as a rear gunner in Stirling bombers. These planes were notorious for their sitting-duck attributes by being prone to attacks from the ground due to their weight and inability to get very high, as well as from airborne attacks. Eventually the inevitable happened and his plane caught fire. The pilot gave the order to bail, but being the rear-gunner, positioned in the tail of the plane, John didn't make it.

He was reported missing in May 1944, his body not being found for another 6 months or more, and then by his uncle in a cemetery in Poix, France.

John's mother and sister were not able to visit the grave until 1947. The grave meanwhile was tended by a local woman, an arrangement made by John's uncle, until the War Grave Commission took over.

This following text was to be published in a book by Ken Gandy who was also a rear gunner, but unfortunately didn't make it into the edited version. 'It was magnificent countryside around Westcott and Oakley, and it was here that Johnny and I became good friends. Johnny Grantham and I had been very friendly since London. We both loved the country and Johnny was going to be a jockey after the war. We would go for walks in the countryside and all would be well until we saw a horse. No matter whether it was a pony, cart horse or race horse, Johnny would be in the field stroking and petting it and they loved it. I would sit and watch. I was no stranger to horses, having been brought up on a farm, and even during school holidays worked with shire horses. To me, however, they were part of the work force, to be fed and cared for so that they could work and pay their way.

Johnny was a gentle person and I began to wonder what he was doing fighting a war. I had seen the devastation caused by bombing in London; had felt sorry for the Londoners sleeping in the Underground and could see London burning from Ely, but this did not affect me to the same extent that Johnny should volunteer to fight the Germans when it was obvious that all he wanted was peace and quiet of his beloved horses. I began to hate the Germans. For me war had finished to be a game. From now on, I recognised war for what it was, and because Germany had plunged the world into war I reasoned that to defeat them would be to restore peace and we could live happily again. Things always seemed so simple to me when I was young.'

Right: the bookcase made in John's memory by Fowlers in Cowfold

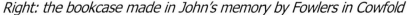

AIR GUNNER'S DEATH
ON BOMBING MISSION

Sgt. J. R. Grantham

Buried in France

Sgt. John Raymond Grantham, younger son of Mr. and Mrs. Tom Grantham, of "Bowshots," West Grinstead, who was previously listed as missing from air operations over Germany, is now officially reported to have lost his life. He is buried in the French cemetery at Poix de la Somme.

Aged 19, Sgt. Grantham was a rear gunner attached to No. 218 (Gold Coast) Squadron. He had been in the R.A.F. fifteen months and had completed fifteen air operations.

Educated at Steyning Grammar School, he was apprenticed to Vic Smythe, the jockey, at Epsom, and had ridden several winners as a steeple-chase jockey. He was keen on hunting and all sports, having ridden since he was three years old, and when on leave from the R.A.F. he rode with the Horsham and Crawley Hunt.

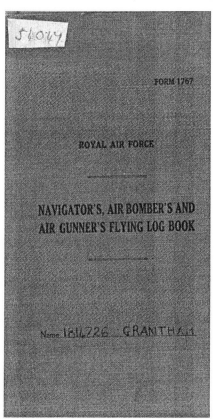

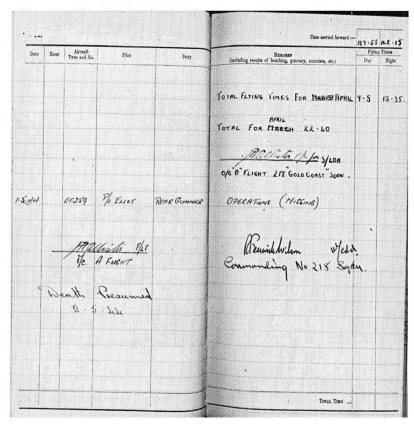

John Grantham's Log Book with its final entry: "Death Presumed 2.5.44"

Other men remembered on the war memorial inside St George's Church:

Harry Flint

Extract from Parish Magazine June 1942:

Mr. Harry Flint, of Dial Post, was laid to rest in West Grinstead Churchyard on May 15th. He had lived a hero's life. But, like most heroes, he was probably unconscious that he was doing anything out of the ordinary. He joined the Navy at the age of 14, but was invalided out during the Great War, after being torpedoed in H.M.S. Gundreda, known as a mystery ship. There were only four survivors. His eyesight was affected by the explosion. He then joined the Merchant Service, and spent 24 years in it. He was torpedoed on the Galway Castle, nine days out of port – also during the Great War. In this ship he was Quartermaster in charge of four lifeboats, and was one of the last to leave the ship. Again he went to sea and was torpedoed in a Union–Castle ship in the Atlantic. Soon after the beginning of the present war he was blown up by a mine off the East Coast in the Dunbar Castle. Immediately he sought another ship. His last voyage was in April, 1941, in the M. V. Hylton. He was torpedoed in the Battle of the Atlantic. For eight hours he was in the water. This long exposure affected his heart. He was sent to hospital, but escaped his doctors and sought another ship. However, the ship's doctor would not pass him. The Union-Castle Line gave him a shore job. He passed quietly into his last port on May 12th, 1942.

Mrs. Flint is very grateful for the sympathy and friendship shown to her on every side, and desires to express her thanks for the many wreaths sent to her.

It is clear from other reports in the parish magazines that Mrs Flint was a tireless fund raiser in Dial Post, raising money for war efforts, prisoners of war and the village hall, amongst other causes.

Fred Budd

Extract from Parish Magazine 1944:

The sympathy of a very large number of friends goes out to the parents and wife of Fred Budd. He was killed in action in Italy while fighting with the Hampshires. Fred was held in very high regard by all who knew him. When the call came, he cheerfully went where duty led him. To do duty well was no new thing to him. He fought through the African campaign, and was awarded the African Star. He wrote cheerfully at all times, and was already looking forward to the return home. A very good "Well done" is written over his life.

Information from the Commonwealth War Grave Commission gives Fred's details as:

Budd, Alfred Arthur
Private   Hampshire Regiment   5th Btn
Aged 32
Date of death   9/11/1944
Serial No   1817433

Son of Arthur Alfred and Mary Ann Budd, husband of Frances Eileen Budd of Partridge Green, Sussex.
Buried in Meldola War Cemetery, Italy

Albert Lucas

Extract from Parish Magazine September 1945:

We much regret to record the death of Albert Lucas, whose home is in Dial Post. He was taken Prisoner of War at Singapore, and went through the experience of the prison camp. He is reported to have died in Thailand in August of this year. His parents can be assured that they have the sympathy of all parishioners. We owe a very great debt to these brave men who endured.

Commonwealth War Grave Commission information:

Lucas, Albert Charles
Sapper   Royal Engineers 41 Fortress Coy
Aged 33
Date of death   4/8/45
Serial No   1873470
(A sapper is another name for private, but particularly in the Royal Engineers)

Son of William and Ada Mary Lucas of Dial Post Sussex.
Kanchanaburi War Cemetery, Thailand

War Memorial in St Michael's Graveyard

William Edwin Sayers

Extracts from Parish Magazines 1944:

The sympathy of the large circle of friends of Mr. and Mrs. Wm. Sayers is with them in the loss of their son, Wm. Edwin, in Italy. He was very highly thought of by those who knew him slightly, and much loved by those who knew him well.

The following letter has been received by Mrs. Sayers from the Officer of the Unit in which William Edwin Sayers served : -

"I received your letter this afternoon, and, as the only remaining officer of Bill's Company, and incidentally his platoon commander at the time of his death, I feel I must answer it immediately. I have also heard from his brother-in-law, Sergt. Brooking, and as soon as I know the locality of the grave, I will write to Bill's wife also. The circumstances of his death were rather tragic. We were moving up for an attack late one afternoon, and prior to making the plan, the Company was dispersed in a gully which appeared quite safe. Shortly afterwards tanks began circulating in the vicinity and drew fire which unfortunately hit us. The spot where Bill was resting behind cover had a direct hit, killing five men altogether.

Bill had been in my platoon for some months, both on the Florence sector and here, and I had consequently had plenty of time and occasion in which to know him well. I can say in all sincerity that he was the very finest type of man and soldier. On duty he was a grand example to us all, fearless, cool in action, and a very faithful N.C.O. to me. He was perpetually cheerful and caring always for the welfare of others – a perfect gentleman at all times, as gentle in his manner as he was smart in his turn-out. He was the very finest type of fellow, for whom I had at all times nothing but the greatest admiration; and I realise only too well how great is the loss you have suffered.

To me he was a terrific loss, for his sterling qualities both as man and soldier inspired us all. Would you please accept my deepest sympathy in your great sorrow, and I will promise to write to his wife as soon as possible.

Commonwealth War Grave Commission information:

Sayers, William Edwin
Private   Somerset Light Infantry   2nd Bn
Aged 29
Date of death   15/9/44
Serial No   6404733

Son of William and Lilian Sayers; husband of Dorothy Rena Sayers of Fittleworth, Sussex
Buried in Coriano Ridge War Cemetery, Italy

Peter Gander

Commonwealth War Grave Commission information:

Gander, Peter Edwin
Sergeant   RAF   229 Sqdn
Aged 22
Date of death   24/12/1943
Serial No   648878

Son of Joseph and Anne Lucy Gander of Partridge Green, Sussex
Commemorated on the Runnymede Memorial near Windsor

Henry Knight

Commonwealth War Grave Commission information:

Knight, Henry George Thomas
Aircraftman 2nd Class   RAF Volunteer Reserve
Aged 21
Date of death   29/11/1943
Serial No   1194884

Son of Herbert Alfred and Caroline Ellen Knight of Partridge Green, Sussex
Commemorated on the Singapore memorial

Douglas Weaver

Commonwealth War Grave Commission information:

Weaver, Douglas Charles
Boy 1st Class Royal Navy HMS Cossack
Aged 17
Date of death   23/10/1941
Serial No   P/JX 177365

Son of Hilda Winifred Weaver, of Partridge Green, Sussex
Commemorated on the Portsmouth Naval Memorial

George Elcock

George Elcock's death was the first reported in the magazines, in December 1941, but I have been unable to find an entry for him on the CWGC's website as yet and he is not on any of the war memorials in the parish. I wonder if Douglas Weaver is in fact George Elcock, or whether their time and circumstances of death are just a coincidence? I haven't found any report of Douglas Weaver at all in the magazines, which considering the loss of such a young man, would surely have mentioned something.

Our very sincere sympathy goes out to Mrs. Elcock and her family. George was one of many who lost his life at sea doing duty on our behalf. Their loss is our common loss. George was a choir-boy, always in his place during his years of service. He was a happy boy, and carried happiness with him. He enjoyed his time at sea, and shared in some of the successes. We shall miss him very much in our village life. In the midst of sorrow there is strength in the memory that the boy had lived a good and useful life, and that he had from his home every encouragement for good.

Margery Cook

Another person mentioned in a magazine for January 1943, but not remembered on any memorial as far as I can tell:

We regret to record the passing away of Margery Cook, aged 23, on Dec.8th. She died at war work in a hospital, and we think of her as one who gave the best she had in order that she might help the common effort. She knew she was not strong, but she determined to do her best, and God took her offering to Himself. Our great sympathy to her parents!

Len Finch   Olive Johnson

Although they are mentioned in the Parish Magazine of 1945 (below) I have not been able to trace any information about these two people. Len Finch appears on the St Michael's memorial so I presume he was a Partridge Green boy and Olive Johnson is mentioned in the parish magazine reports but is not on any memorial.

In our rejoicings we remember with gratitude Peter Gander, Henry Knight, George Elcock, Len Finch, William Edwin Sayers, Claude Mitchell, John Grantham and Olive Johnson, who went from this parish and gave their lives for us. We remember also those who are nearest and dearest to them.

Partridge Green Methodist Chapel

By Norman Berry

Below are extracts from the book "100 Not Out" published in 2006 on the Church's centenary by kind permission of the Church.

Interior of the Chapel as it was during the War

Rev. Cyril Hunwick became minister in 1938 and remained through the difficult early war years until 1942.

The hall completed in 1932 and intended as a Sunday School, being in a strategic position in the centre of the village, was now in great demand. In the early part of the war it was used as an evacuees school during the day and a canteen for locally billeted soldiers in the evening. Being a fairly new building it was very popular in the very cold winter of 1941 when many of the older local buildings were cold and draughty (see poem facing).

Rev. Ernest Livesley became minister in 1942 and the hall was used in alternate weeks for United Churches midweek services with the other village denominations.

Below are extracts of letters received by the organist Mrs. Jackson in 1959. These were in response to appeals for funds for a new organ but also for memories of the chapel's history.

Memories to Mrs. Jackson from David and Joan Anderson of Caterham, dated 25 January 1959

Our memories of Partridge Green are very happy ones in spite of the difficulties of the war years. The Staples family was our first contact when Reg Staples dug our car out of a ditch in the blackout. Mr. Staples looked after us like a father and Mrs. Staples coloured our life with the most beautiful flowers and the rosiest of apples.

It is a comforting thing to look back sometimes and see how much friendship and fun warmed the long dark days of constant uncertainty and fear.

Harvest festivities with Mrs. Green proudly producing the finest pampas grass for the pulpit. Old Mrs. Sherlock digging her potatoes and persuading her Roman Catholic neighbour to carry them into the Methodist chapel for her, such a twinkle in her eye too. Mr. Whatley with his beautiful white hair and noble head; Doris with her beaming smile singing away whether the organ wheezed or burst forth into unexpected treble descants.

The many soldiers who enjoyed the canteen and came to worship on Sunday — sometimes so tired that they slept gently on the hymn book ledge through the prayers and then woke smiling only to nod again when the sermon began and we sat in silence before the bombers began to drone over Shoreham Gap on their way to London.

Letter to Friends at Partridge Green from Rev. Cyril Hunwick dated 23 January 1959

It does seem a long while since I was with you. To be exact it was from 1938 to 1942. Unfortunately the clouds of war were upon us for three out of those four years. I remember during that time the steadfast loyalty of you all and the happy fellowship we had together. I also remember the kindly hospitality offered to me at all times in your homes and quite a number of memories will live with me that perhaps one cannot put down in so many words.

Poem by G A Lambert

of the 38th Signal Division

A big crowd in the local canteen,
Run by the ladies of Partridge Green
Lots of activity, plenty of noise,
Made by the 38th Div. Sigs. Boys.
A few of the lads at the piano sing,
Eats and drinks the ladies bring.
They come with trays around the room,
Loaded with things that soldiers consume.
We sure appreciate what they do,
That they work hard is really true.
Table-tennis, draughts and darts
Are being played in various parts
Of the room which holds a crowd
Of chaps who shout and sing aloud.
Piano music fills the air,
Various pianists do their share

On the jolliest evening there has been
In the Methodist Hall at Partridge Green.

Memory to Mrs. Jackson from Rev. Ernest and Mrs. Bertha Livesley of Hitchin, dated 1959

Your circular letter brought back many very happy memories of our years in the Horsham and Dorking circuit and especially of the good times we had at Partridge Green. Although it was wartime (and often after a midweek fellowship meeting I waited for an overdue last train to Horsham held up by an air raid at Brighton!) and most eatables were rationed, it made no difference to the generous hospitality of the Partridge Green Methodists.

My wife has reminded me of the enthusiastic meeting held in the chapel at which a branch of the Women's Work for Overseas Missions was formed, followed later by a very successful garden meeting at which Mrs. Webb Anderson took the chair.

Local Travel during the War

By Julie Beck

To find out more about how people got about during the war I started off by going to see a couple who were married soon after the war ended in 1945. The ceremony was at West Blatchington on the coast near Brighton, the bride Doris Lynn being born and bred in the area and her bridegroom Fred Monnery a cowman at Needs Farm in Partridge Green. They made their home in West Grinstead, where they still live.

Doris and Fred Monnery in 1947

Doris, who lived in Hove during most of the war, used to travel up to Fred on the bus, or on occasion cycle. She remembers cycling to Henfield one time when the group of Girls Guildry from her local church were camping at the school there. She wasn't camping herself as she was working, but on the weekend she and a couple of others cycled up to the camp. Doris was sporting a rather nice backless frock at the time and managed to get told off for her attire. On the way home she also got a puncture and had to walk some of the way back, so possibly not the best way to have spent her day off!

Towards the end of the war both Fred and Doris used the buses to get to see one another, choosing the bus over the train or vice versa depending on where and when they were going. The buses ran far more frequently than now, and of course trains ran even more frequently than now, both filled to capacity.

	HORSHAM, MAPLEHURST, WEST GRINSTEAD, PARTRIDGE GREEN AND STEYNING	
80	With connections at Steyning to and from Brighton.	**80**

		NS	NS	NS	SO			
Horsham (Carfax)	...	8 0	10 0	1 0	1 0	4 0	6 0	8 45	...
Horsham Station	...	8 2	10 2	1 2	1 2	4 2	6 3	8 47	...
Mannings Heath	...	8 11	1011	1 11	1 11	4 11	6 13	8 57	...
Monks Gate ...	...	8 14	1014	1 14	1 14	4 14	6 16	9 0	...
Nuthurst	...	8 18	1018	1 18	1 18	4 18	6 20	9 5	...
Maplehurst	...	8 23	1023	1 23	1 23	4 23	6 26	9 10	...
Champions Gate	...	...	1028	1 28	...	4 28	6 31	9 16	...
West Grinstead Station	...	...	1030	1 30	...	4 30	6 34	9 18	...
West Grinstead Priory	...	...	1034	1 34	...	4 34	6 38	9 23	...
Littleworth ...	...	...	1038	1 38	...	4 38	6 42	9 27	...
Partridge Green	...	...	1041	1 41	...	4 41	6 46	9 30	...
Ashurst	...	...	1049	1 49	...	4 49	6 54	9 39	...
Wiston Road	...	...	1056	1 56	...	4 56	7 2	9 47	...
Steyning (White Horse)	...	...	11 0	2 0	...	5 0	7 6	9 51	...
Steyning	dep	...	11 3	2 3	...	5 3	7 10	9 52	...
Shoreham	arr	...	1119	2 19	...	5 19	7 27	10 9	...
Brighton	,,	...	1146	2 46	...	5 46	7 57	1039	...

		NS	NS	NS	SO			
Brighton	dep	...	8 20	1020	...	1 20	4 20	6 22	...
Shoreham	,,	...	8 44	1047	...	1 47	4 47	6 52	...
Steyning	arr	...	9 0	11 3	...	2 3	5 3	7 10	...

			NS	NS	NS	SO			
Steyning (White Horse)	...	...	9 0	11 3	...	2 3	5 3	7 10	...
Wiston Road	...	...	9 4	11 7	...	2 7	5 7	7 14	...
Ashurst ...	...	...	9 10	1114	...	2 14	5 14	7 22	...
Partridge Green	...	...	9 17	1122	...	2 22	5 22	7 30	...
Littleworth ...	...	...	9 19	1124	...	2 24	5 24	7 33	...
West Grinstead Priory	...	...	9 23	1128	...	2 28	5 28	7 37	...
West Grinstead Station	...	...	9 26	1131	...	2 31	5 31	7 40	...
Champions Gate	...	...	9 28	1133	...	2 33	5 33	7 43	...
Maplehurst ...	...	8 27	9 32	1138	1 38	2 38	5 38	7 48	...
Nuthurst ...	...	8 33	9 38	1143	1 43	2 43	5 43	7 54	...
Monks Gate ...	...	8 37	9 42	1147	1 47	2 47	5 47	7 58	...
Mannings Heath	...	8 40	9 45	1150	1 50	2 50	5 50	8 1	...
Horsham Station	...	8 48	9 53	1158	1 58	2 58	5 58	8 10	...
Horsham (Carfax)	...	8 50	9 55	12 0	2 0	3 0	6 0	8 12	...

NS—Not Sundays.   SO—Sundays Only.

Part of the bus timetable issued on 3rd January 1943

A lot of people used the bus to get around locally; in the parish magazine for June 1942 travel arrangements were well in place before the event of a Mother's Union trip to Westlands, just to the north east of the junction with Littleworth Lane and the A272:

'Another date to note down is July 23rd when we are invited to Westlands to meet Mrs. Polhill and her guests – the elderly evacuees from London. Many of us can recall delightful afternoons in previous years in Miss Thynne's home. We are asked to bring our own food, but tea will be provided. Westlands is not far from Champions Corner on No. 80 Bus Route. We propose to go by the bus which leaves Partridge Green at 2.20p.m., and West Grinstead Priory Corner at 2.26.'

The previous year's Mother's Union trip was a little further afield but still on the No. 80 bus: 'Our Committee suggested that, as a Summer Outing was desirable, we might take the opportunity of going to see the Gardens at Sedgwick Park, which are open to the public on payment of 1s. on July 24th. Our return fare on No. 80 bus would be 10d. It was suggested that each of us take a picnic tea, and that we travel by the No. 80 bus due to leave Partridge Green at 2.20 p.m., and returning from Nuthurst at 6.22 p.m.'

Back to Fred at the farm; goods to and from the farm went mainly by lorry during the war, although sometimes the train was used depending on the destination (livestock were known to have been transported from markets either at Steyning or sometimes Chichester to get to the farm). Sometimes Fred would grab a lift with the milk lorry down to Hove to see Doris, then catch a bus to Corner House at Shermanbury and walk the rest of the way home.

Fred's family, like most at that time, didn't have a car, as only those who could afford it had cars. The usual mode of private transport was bicycle. Fred cycled to work, to the village, to train stations and they usually cycled for a day out, reaching places like Littlehampton in a few hours.

Fuel for what cars there were was also rationed but Fred doesn't recall there being too much problem on the farm to get fuel for the tractors and other engines, but then the farm and its workers got extra rations on cheese and butter amongst other things.

The farmer Fred worked for had relatively free movement, providing he had a reason for his travel, ie taking stock to market or picking up feed etc. Graham Beck recalls his father Louis telling a story about one such trip to Shoreham when he took Graham's aunt with him. Usually there was no problem passing any checkpoints, but this day they faced a minor interrogation because the aunt had no need to be travelling with him.

During the war no-one was allowed to show a light after dark, you didn't dare. The cars all had masked headlights, nothing more, and the houses all had black outs at the windows. Not only the houses. Fred recalls the farm being reprimanded one time when a light in the milking parlour could be seen across the fields at Dial Post!

One tale Fred tells starts with him cycling to work, "I'd just set off early one morning to get to Needs to do the milking, it was still dark, very dark. I was peddling along when I hears this puffing behind me 'pouf pouf pouf'. Well, I thought someone was following me, scared the living daylights out of me so I peddled faster and faster uphill towards Needs, still this 'pouf pouf pouf' getting louder. I rushed in past the front gate and leaped off to shut it behind me and peddled like fury to get to the farm and still I could hear this 'pouf pouf pouf' only now it was in front of me. You know what it was? The steam train heading off!" I guess that just shows how dark it was and how frightening it could be.

Although goods were still under ration when the couple got married, Doris' job working for the Belgravia dairy meant she had friends able to get them what they wanted for their wedding, exchanging coupons to help make the day special. With Doris' contacts in the dairy and Fred on the farm they feel they never went short during the war, but of course their way of living before, during and after war broke out was not like mine or theirs now.

Groceries came via a van from Southwater, bakery goods from Cowfold and also a sweet van came visiting once a week. Your order would go in the week before, and pretty much every week you had the same things, but the vans would carry surplus items you could go and choose from when it pulled up, providing you had your coupons of course. You could also visit the local grocery store in the village during the war, if you could carry your purchases home!

You'd think it was pretty quiet up at Park Lane, not much going on? But that's not so with the Canadian soldiers in the Park, who were often seen or heard marching along the roads, whether just on patrol or en route to somewhere important. At West Grinstead Lodge, just north of the Catholic Church in Park Lane the army had a pigeon loft, used for sending messenger birds, again who knows where? So there was often something to be seen. One time Fred remembers seeing six or seven coaches parked up at the church end of the lane, finding out later that they were waiting to pick up Italian Prisoners of War from West Grinstead station and transport them to Jendens Farm out at Shipley where they had a camp.

Someone else I talked to who did drive during the war was Di Holman whose family, the Granthams, lived near West Grinstead Station. Before the war Di cycled to Cowfold for school whilst her brothers John and Tony cycled to Jolesfield. When they were older they caught the train to head down the line, through the brooks south of Henfield, which, when flooded, were like going across the sea, to Steyning Grammar School.

By the age of 17 Di was driving errands for her father. Her mother didn't drive so she became a capable dogsbody running to the bank or shops or wherever. When war broke out she volunteered to drive for the Women's Voluntary Service, taking expectant mothers from the locality to a Rest Home. She remembers this could be quite interesting as she only had a small car, a Fiat 500 and she often had trouble getting the heavily laden ladies in and out of the car.

She also drove to Horsham collecting goodies such as cigarettes and chocolates from the WVS Headquarters in Hurst Road Horsham and running them out to the local army camps. Later in the war she would move to London and drive an ambulance there. Every six weeks or so Di would be officially allowed leave to go home. She'd get a travel warrant and come back by train. On those days when she had time off and the local Hunt were riding she'd hitchhike home. She says this was all perfectly safe and I guess with the rationing of fuel people were far more likely to double up on their travel and share transport.

The memories of another local resident Claire Walton (née Campbell) who lived in Park Lane also mention transport during the war:

'The black out was very strictly enforced, as everywhere, and this applied to trains, buses and cars lights as well. The latter consisted of a cap (metal) with slits across and fixed over car headlights. They allowed little light to be projected immediately in front of the vehicle and this illuminated a short distance ahead. I am sure today this would be considered very dangerous – it was amazing how people found their way around, especially if they didn't know their route. Maps were taboo as was everything likely to give information of their whereabouts to an invader. Road signs and directions (also many street names) were removed and the names of some shops and pubs on which appeared the locality eg West Grinstead Parish church, were also removed or blacked out with thick paint. This also had drawbacks when travelling by public transport as one had to rely on a helpful conductor or driver – or trust to luck.

Later in the war my husband and I had a small car but I could seldom use it, petrol coupons were saved for special events, like leaves, the ration being 3 – 6 gallons per month, depending on the size of your car engine. Later in the war, around D-Day, there was no petrol at all for civilian use and those who had hung on to their pet ponies and traps certainly scored – as did anyone who had a horse and could ride.'

Wartime Cars...

Some cars which may have been familiar around the parish before, during and soon after the Second World War:

Winnie Bryon (née Jenkins) with her Austin 7

Winnie won some money in a competition and bought the car to get her to work in Worthing.

Mr and Mrs Gumbrill with their Model T Ford

The Gumbrills ran the blacksmiths in Bines Road and worked closely with the neighbouring wheelwrights, so I suppose it was inevitable that they had a car.

Cars didn't really develop in any way over the war years, as no time or money could be directed towards inessential motoring, so there were a lot of very much pre-war vehicles on the road during the war and long after.

The shapes however did change a year or so after the end of the war, the old square bodies replaced by curves and the headlamps incorporated into the bonnet. Although in 1946 all cars still had the facility to start them with a handle, most were sophisticated enough to have electric starters even before the war.

I don't know about you, but my car today is comfortable, warm when needed and cool when needed. It has smooth gear changes and travels along at 70 mph with ease. Not so back in the war years. Most cars had hard and lumpy seats, doors that didn't quite seal resulting in the inevitable draught and odd dribble (or in some cases soakings) of rain.

Top speeds…. forget your 70 mph, try 50 mph with a nice vibration and rattle of all and every part. What about in-car stereo? No. You had to buy a special licence if you wanted a radio in your car even up until the early sixties. Power steering? Power assisted braking? Don't be silly.

Cynthia Baker, née Shackell, leaning on a 1946 Austin 12HP
outside Belmordean Cottages in the 1960s

Driving licences were introduced in 1903 and given to anyone who applied. No driving test or check on medical fitness was required. Minimum age for riding motorcycles was 14 and 17 for other vehicles.   Pictured below is Louis Beck's driving licence wallet. Although we know Louis (born in 1900) would have been driving from an early age, his first licence dates from only 1931.

The wallet is full of these licences. Each year the licence was renewed and shown by a slip of paper stuck one on top of the other, added into the thick red card wallet, the same shape and size as the ID cards (about 4" by 2½").   This renewing continued in this format through the war, but I found it interesting that although driving tests, which were introduced in 1935, were suspended through the war, poor old Louis (and everyone else) still had to go and get their licence renewed every year, and pay 5s over to West Sussex County Council for the privilege!

The list of permitted vehicles on the inside cover refers to a 1947 act, but even then the vehicles mentioned sound quite fun; 'heavy locomotive', 'heavy motor car', 'motor tricycle equipped with any means for reversing', 'trolley vehicle', 'mowing machine or vehicle controlled by a pedestrian' and lastly, I think of 'invalid carriage' as being a fairly modern invention, but it's there listed under the 'Groups of Vehicles'.   Of course, if you look closely into today's licence the same vehicles are listed (not sure about the 'locomotives') and grouped similarly, so nothing much has really changed, but aren't we lucky not to have to renew *our* licences today, and no, it hasn't been replaced by road tax; that was introduced in 1910.

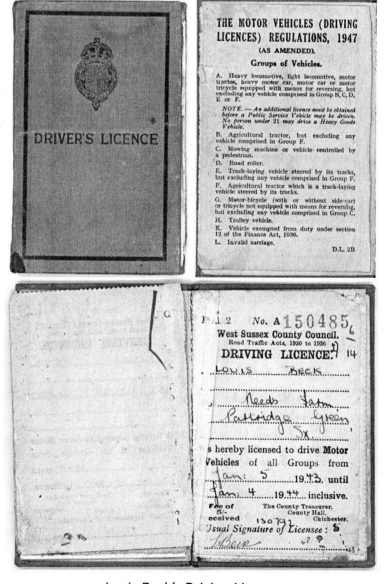

Louis Beck's Driving Licence

Other information from DVLA website: 'A Trip Down Motoring Lane'

Policing

By Colin Rudling

P.C. Charlie Holdstock was the Village Policeman throughout the war years. He was assisted by a number of Police Auxiliaries, including Herbert Mitchell, a farmer and the local butcher, who was the senior Auxiliary Officer.

Charles was born in Hastings in 1894. On leaving school he became a smiths mate, but in 1914, aged twenty, he joined the Police Force and was stationed at Arundel.

When war broke out in 1914 he wrote to his Superintendent asking for permission to join Lord Kitchener's Army as he felt "It is my duty to do so". Permission was granted and Charlie joined the Coldstream Guards. He was taken prisoner by the Germans and sent to work in the salt mines. At the end of the war, after serving four years and 179 days in the Army, and at the age of twenty five he rejoined the Police. Around 1920 Charlie married May Linfield of Billingshurst. A year or so later he came to Partridge Green, where he remained until he retired in 1946.

Holly Cottage (above), almost opposite the entrance to the King George V playing field, was the Police House and there the Holdstock family grew up: Eric, the eldest, who later joined the Police and rose to the rank of Superintendent, Betty, Maisie, and the youngest, John.

In 1936 Charlie's pay was £4 15s (£4.75); in 1941 he had a rise of 16s 7d (83p), non pensionable. By 1945 his pay had risen to £6 3s (£6.15), which was probably around 20% more than a skilled craftsman would earn in this area at that time.

To collect his pay Charlie had to cycle to Horsham Police Station once a fortnight. He must have covered many thousands of miles on his bicycle, as it was his only means of patrolling his large rural beat. Sometimes he would be accompanied by dog belonging to Herbert Mitchell called Tatters, a mongrel, which due to an old injury, ran on only three legs.

Almost every family would have been known personally by him, and very little went on that he wasn't aware of.

Sometimes he would have his shotgun wrapped in a sack and tied to his crossbar when out on his beat, just in case he had the opportunity to bag a rabbit or two. My father, Jim Rudling, would often tell of the time when he was installing a cattle trough in a field off Littleworth Lane. Being startled by a gun blast and the sound of shot whooshing over his head, he looked over the hedge and there was Charlie astride his bike with shotgun in hand, "Oh hallo Jim, would you mind picking up that bird for me?" Whereupon Charlie continued on his patrol.

Pub landlords would leave a drink outside on the step when they knew he would be coming by on patrol.

The following is an extract from the memoirs of Cecil Longhurst:-

" Policemen in those days stopped all their duty in one place. Charlie, well he'd been at Partridge Green a good few years. He liked quite a lot of drink, course, he wasn't supposed to drink on the beat. What he would do, well there wasn't a phone, he'd have to go to certain phone boxes at certain times and ring in to the Superintendent.

He used to come in to us quite often as we had a fire going most times. He could always find out what he needed, but he didn't dare go into a pub. He'd look in the window and them inside would say "there's old Charlie outside, better take him a drink" So they'd take him out a drink and talk to him outside. Well the Superintendent knew what Charlie was up to, but he could never catch him. One night he thought he'd catch him up at the Tabby Cat. Sure enough there was old Holdstock, drink in hand. But Charlie, he just passed it to the bloke what had just brought it out and made out he'd just been interviewing him".

PC Holdstock's courage and strength were both dramatically demonstrated when, whilst delivering police circulars to Blanches Farm Littleworth, he heard a cry for help coming from the stock house. He found the farm manager, Mr Fulcher being attacked by an enraged bull pinning him into a corner. With his bare hands PC Holdstock manhandled the bull allowing Mr Fulcher to escape, without doubt saving his life. PC Holdstock received a commendation for bravery award for his actions.

A young John Hawkins was sitting outside The Hare and Hounds in Cowfold, while father Harry was inside enjoying a lunchtime drink. He watched with interest as PC Holdstock rode up on his bike, lent it against the wall, removed his tunic, folded it neatly over the handlebars, removed his hat and placed it on top of the jacket, took off his cycle clips and clipped them onto the crossbar, carefully rolled up his shirt sleeves and walked into the pub. Seconds later, one after the other, three drunken French Canadian soldiers came flying through the doorway landing in a heap at the bottom of the steps. Military Police then arrived, threw them into a lorry and drove off. I can well imagine that Charlie would then have enjoyed a pint on the house for his trouble.

Petrol was very hard to come by during the War, motorcycles were popular because they were more economical than cars, but received a similar ration. Harry Hawkins had a large "Indian" motorcycle and to increase the seating capacity from two to four a plank of wood was lashed to the saddle and Harry with three friends would ride down to Brighton; Charlie was often one of the passengers.

On VE Day Charlie led a parade of Police Auxiliaries and Partridge Green Home Guard from Shermanbury Grange up the High Street along Church Road to Mill Lane, down Littleworth Lane and back to Shermanbury Grange.

PC Charlie Holdstock was a remarkable man who commanded respect and affection in equal measure. He is fondly remembered by everyone fortunate enough to have known him.

Partridge Green Home Guard

By Colin Rudling

The Home Guard unit at Partridge Green was called C Company, 4th. Sussex Home Guard and was commanded by Col. Watson, who lived at Wymarks Shermanbury. Their Headquarters were the hut behind The Partridge, which was until recently The Wool Shop.

The main job of the unit was to defend the road bridge over the railway line; this had been identified by the military as a "Nodal" point, that is one which must be defended at all costs. They also patrolled the village in pairs throughout the night.

Although the LDV (Local Defence Volunteers), later the Home Guard, were the butt of many a joke at the time (and still are right up to the present day), the truth was that, particularly in this part of the country, very few would survive if an invasion came. They had little chance against a well armed and trained enemy; their job was to engage and delay them for as long as possible, forcing the enemy to deploy some of their troops to fight them, giving our regular army more time to organise counter attacks. They knew the enemy would not be taking prisoners in the early stages of an invasion.

In those early days they had no uniforms or rifles, but several had, or had access to shot guns. They were issued with twelve bore cartridges which, instead of lead shot, had a single lead ball as the projectile, not as effective as a rifle at long range, but lethal close up. As the threat of invasion faded some replaced the single ball with lead shot and deployed the ammunition against the local rabbit population.

The Postmaster, Mr Frederick Cyril Fisher, who had been in the Royal Flying Corps during WW1, was a member of the Post Office Home Guard. He was issued with an overcoat and a bayonet, but no rifle. Mr Fisher had orders that, should the invasion come, he must bury all Postal Orders and the Post Office stamp in a hole in the garden.

The "Tinker" Tailor brothers, Steve and Tom, who lived in a shed surrounded by piles of junk on Jolesfield Common, were very popular members of the Home Guard, as they always arrived for the night shift equipped with a bottle or two of their home made wine.

Two members of the troop were commended for their bravery in rescuing a German pilot whose Me109 fighter had crashed in flames at Plummers Plain. Tommy Child of South Street, Partridge Green, Charles Gardener of Littleworth, aided by local farm worker Frank Burgess, were all working in the area at the time. They all rushed to the stricken plane and dragged the pilot clear in spite of great danger from exploding ammunition. He was however badly burnt and died from his injuries the next day.

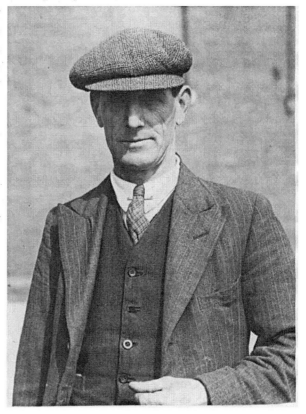

Thankfully for the Home Guard, and the rest of us, invasion never came, but the Partridge Green troop did fall victim to "friendly fire". On the fourth anniversary of their formation a detachment from the troop was training on a firing range on the Downs above Steyning when

Right: Tommy Child in 1948, one of 3 men awarded commendations for the rescue of a German pilot from his burning Me109 at Plummers Plain

some shells fell amongst them. Pte. L. T. Wylie of Maplehurst was killed, Cpl. J. Lindfield also of Maplehurst was seriously injured. The detachment was under the command of Lt. H. A. Greenwood, a schoolmaster living at Five Acres Partridge Green who was severely injured in both legs.

Lt. Greenwood arrived at Partridge Green at the beginning of the War as headmaster of the evacuated Brixton School By the time of the accident he was again teaching in London but remained a local resident and in command of his platoon. Col. Watson said: "Lt. Greenwood is a particularly keen officer. Wylie was one of the keenest members of the company". Shortly afterwards there was another casualty when Cpl. Sparkes (of Dial Post) collapsed on parade and died soon afterwards; he is commemorated on the War Graves Commission Memorial in Ashington Churchyard.

Dial Post Home Guard

Extract from Bicycles, Bells, Bombers and Bees by Julie Beck
Tales from Cecil Longhurst

"Well, they put out an appeal over the wireless and then a couple of days later somebody came round and they started the Home Guard at Dial Post. You didn't have to do it. I'd already been told I wouldn't get called up 'cause even then they classed my deafness as severe. Lt Daniels, I said to him I was rather deaf, he said never mind you'll probably be able to help us. They hadn't got many then. Quite a few from the 1914 War joined when they heard it on the wireless, there was no organisation though. When I decided to do it, I think that was at the weekend and then it started the next week at Dial Post Village Hall.

All we had for several months after we joined was a khaki arm band with LDV on, Local Defence Volunteer. When the home guard started they'd got virtually nothing.

It was after a lot had come back from Dunkirk, well a lot of them came back, they didn't have all of the uniform, they might have had trousers, they might not have got their battle dress, hardly any of them had their rifles. Some of them might have had two rifles. Well they was lined up close to the sea; I know one or two chaps said the chap next to them would say hold on to my rifle for a few minutes, well before the chap got back there was a space on a boat see, so he went on with two rifles.

It wouldn't have mattered if a lot of the Home Guard had any weapons at all. It used to be amusing to me, used to get people come round doing lectures you see, we had nothing to deal with tanks, no armour piercing bullets or anything. They said the only way to deal with the tanks was to fire at the joint between the turret and the hole. I doubt if half of the chaps could hit the tank at 25 yards let alone anything else.

Funny, a lot of people have been asking about Dial Post Home Guard. Someone put a letter in the paper asking if anyone had a photograph of the guard; well, I only know of one person having a photograph, that's Mrs Bean. Well, there weren't many photos 'cause one, it was wartime and you wasn't really meant to take photos of anything and two, there wasn't any film about to take them with. I had a camera but no film.

We only ever arrested one man. Well, the chap stopping people as they came through the village had this man with no ID. He said he was supposed to be going to Rustington from Crawley. Well we didn't know what else to do, him not having any ID or anything so we arrested him. Well, our Commanding Officer, old Daniels took him to the Police Station at Horsham. Normally we wouldn't have known what happened to him and that, but Charlie Holdstock, the local policeman, he had to be at the phone box in Dial Post at a certain time and then the phone box in Shipley so I s'pose he had an hour or two to spare and used to come talk to us. He said the chap was grumbling and moaning about being picked up and that he had to get to Rustington and being all suspicious and that, he had 36 gold sovereigns on him. Well nobody had much more than 1 or 2 usually, so they kept him all night. He gave an address of a woman in Crawley who'd vouch for him. When they found her she said, 'oh dear, he got in trouble? I been on at him scores of times to get an ID card'. She confirmed that he had a sister in Rustington, but strange thing was he lived in a sort of shed near this woman, obviously not been through military hands at all. Well he had a beard, but he didn't seem that old, but he wasn't a 5th columnist by all accounts."

When Cecil started with the Home Guard, he started off on patrol from a shepherd's hut near Wincaves, his patrol taking him down to Bay Bridge, back up Rook Cross, down to Hobshorts and along Sands Lane back to Dial Post. "Bob Greenfield who I went with, he, well he did have a rifle, he only had 5 rounds of ammunition, he didn't have a uniform, he only had an armband. I didn't have anything except the armband. The two of us were looking for parachute troops with one rifle and five rounds, they said if you do see parachute troops, don't engage them, try to get back and report it, but with 5 rounds it wouldn't have been much of an engagement, good job we didn't find any."

The hut being small and not very winter friendly it was abandoned in favour of the house recently used as the Pepper Mill in the heart of Dial Post. It was often used by the army with different troops staying one or two nights on their way to somewhere else. It was certainly warmer and unlike the shepherd's hut, less likely to blow away in a gale. It had the added bonus of being just down the road from the pub, a frequent haunt of some of the men allegedly.

"We used to do, well I s'pose looking back Lt Daniels in charge had to do something to justify his position, and on this Sunday morning, he divided up the people there: half defended Dial Post and half had to attack and try to take the HQ. Well course, the people that was defending, their sergeant was old Bill Elleker. He sort of took the view that nobody would be able to get into Dial Post if he put people on the road that way and the other way. Well my sergeant, old Jock Martin he was pretty wily, he thought of things that other people didn't think. He took us down the road towards Ashington. Somebody said, well we was sat by the side of the road, what are we going to do? Wait for the bus. Wait for the bus? Yeah, we'll go up to Dial Post on the bus. Somebody said they'll see us. Not if we get down on the floor they won't.

So we waited for the bus to come along, Jock, well he told the driver what he wanted and he laughed and took us on. We could see the blokes either side of the road as we went up on the bus down near where the nursery is now. They didn't take any notice of us though. When we got up to the garage Jock said to the driver 'can you drop us here and not at the stop', then we was very nearly outside the garden gate of the guard room, nobody about, nobody about at all. We got closer and heard some talking and laughter inside. We walked in and there was three blokes sitting on a desk, their rifles leaning up against the wall so we took them prisoner. Bill Elleker, he'd gone down the pub."

I asked Cecil if he enjoyed his time in the Home Guard, "well, not much really, I was too darned tired. During that summer when we had most to do, we had harvesting to do in the Park. That wasn't our job like, but we left off painting and that and helped out on the farm. Course, with the war everybody had lost a lot of workers and everything was pretty much manual work. I had to go round stacking the sheaves ready for the threshing machine. It took a whole day to go right round the outside of the Park stacking these sheaves. You'd start at 8.30 in the morning. You couldn't start earlier cause it was too wet, but you wouldn't finish until 8.30 at night, then I had to get to Dial Post for 9, so no, I didn't really enjoy it as such."

Life in the Home Guard

By Reg Staples

Reg Staples (writes Graham Beck) was a well known and liked farmer in Partridge Green and spent his time in the Home Guard as a medic and Non-Commissioned Officer; being in a reserved occupation on the farm, he was not called up. After the war he was inspired by the BBC programme 'Dad's Army' to tell his own story to local groups such as the WI. The following is from a transcript of one of his talks and joins it as the guard go for shooting practice at the brickyard which used to be to the west of the railway line opposite the Partridge (where Sussex Farm is now).

In the brickyard there was a pit and a bank where they had been digging the clay and the target was set up by this bank for us to fire at. I noticed with that on top of the bank somebody had started an allotment. It was Fred the village postman and of course we had a dig for victory campaign at the beginning of the war and Fred had got hold of some manure from some farmer nearby and he'd got some of the most luxuriant potato greens I had ever seen, they were about 3ft high, there they were, right on the top of this bank where Fred had grown them.

And so we lined up and the sergeant began to tell us about these weapons. "First of all" he said "you'll notice they don't have triggers, they've got two buttons, button A and button B. You press button A and there's a single shot. You press button B and then it goes on bang bang bang bang bang until all the cartridges are used". Then he pointed out to us that to start using them you clipped on a magazine which contained about a dozen cartridges and he said, "Pressing button B it will keep going until they're all used. You don't fire this from your shoulder, you fire it from your hip" and so he began to demonstrate and he pressed button A. The machine started, but it

Reg Staples of Joles Farm in what is now Staples Hill, near St Michael's.

didn't just fire one shot, it fired the whole lot! After he'd had one or two tries he said "well I think perhaps these guns, well, button A doesn't work, you'll have to reconcile yourself that whichever button you press the whole magazine is going to go off and you won't be able to stop it".

So first the sergeant had a go; he was a First World War man but he'd never handled a gun like this, fumbling just a bit, pressed button A, and off went the gun, it shook and rattled and trembled. He didn't hit the target, neither did the second man and then it was my turn.

Now, I'd never fired anything like this of course, but I had seen in a gangster film somewhere that there were men who used this kind of weapon, firing from the hip and I remembered that they had gone round in half a circle, so I thought now if I just press this button and go round in half a circle I'm bound to hit something. So that's what I did. I pressed button A and the thing started, ooh it rattled, it shook and kicked and trembled and I did my best to hold on to it. Well, I went round in a half circle alright and when all the bullets had gone out the sergeant he emitted a cry of triumph, "Yes" he said "you've hit the target, oh but my, just look at those potatoes".

You know, I'd mowed half those potato greens the whole length of the row as though a hedge trimmer had gone along and cut them down. I never heard what sort of a crop Fred the village postman had, nothing was ever said about it and I didn't make any enquiries either, but in the end the sergeant said to us, "Well you make a very good first aid man but you don't know much about guns do you?" and so we admitted that we didn't know anything about this sort of gun anyway. Well, do you know, we carried those guns with us wherever we went, right throughout the war, they always went where we went when we were in uniform, and never again did they let us have any ammunition to fire them and we never again used them or pressed button A again, not during the whole of the war.

Well, after that now with our arms, our equipment was complete and it was only a few Sundays after that Vic Greenwood said to us "Next Sunday we're going to have a somewhat more ambitious exercise, we're going to attack Cowfold". Now Cowfold was the next village along the road to Horsham, about 3 miles away, and the Home Guard at Cowfold were going to defend the village and Partridge Green Home Guard were going to attack and see if they could capture the village. And he said "I shall want the first aid men to be there because there might be casualties, you must bring your stretcher a few blankets, first aid kit" and so on.

Now, Cowfold is a village a little bit smaller than Partridge Green with one long more or less straight street and at the bottom end there's the Bridge Garage, by the Bridge Garage there's a stream and then the road goes gently up hill for about quarter of a mile, right to the top of Cowfold. We discovered that the first aid post was on the highest point, at the top of Cowfold and we were stationed down by the Bridge Garage.

It was very interesting, there were bangs and run-ins and fighting and so on, and the old ladies going to church wondered what on earth had come to Cowfold that Sunday morning. We stood around and waited when suddenly there was a cry "First aid men there's a casualty" and so we went running with our stretcher. And sure enough there he was, lying on the ground.

I recognised him, it was George. George was the cowman at the next farm to mine and George was sixteen stone. When he saw us he grinned and I looked at him and said "Goodness it would be you wouldn't it" , he said "Yes, I'm sure I'm going to enjoy this". I knew what we'd got to do, we'd got to carry him a quarter of a mile right through the middle of Cowfold, up hill all the way. He said, "Come on, undo the stretcher and I'll jump on" and I said "No, don't you do that, you lay still, you don't know who might be watching, we'll lift you on properly", and so we did. We put him on the stretcher, we wrapped him up in blankets and we picked him up and off we went, four of us, one at each corner and the corporal bringing up the rear.

We hadn't got very far before Henry (one of the stretcher bearers) suddenly said "Why are you going so fast, I can't keep up, you're forgetting my bad heart". We slowed down a bit, and of course in those days there was very little traffic and so we walked along in the middle of the road up this slope towards the first aid post. A little farther again there was a cry from Henry "Slower, slower I can't keep up". Well eventually he got so puffed we had to put George down in the middle of the road and the corporal said "Here look, I'll take one corner, you walk behind, just try and look important and keep up". And so off we went.

We reached the top of the hill eventually, a little bit puffed but we got our casualty there. Then we turned up a carriage drive, to a small mansion. The lady and gentleman who lived there had placed their house at the disposal of the Home Guard that Sunday morning. So in we went, through a French window onto a most beautiful carpet and there we put George down, stretcher and all, in front of the doctor.

The doctor was old Doctor Dickins. He was our doctor and I knew him very well and of course he was an officer. So, we uncovered George and there he was. Now for some reason best known to George he had worn that morning a brilliant scarlet pullover underneath his battledress and when the doctor undid his battledress and began to see what was wrong with him, I thought , as I knew the doctor so well, perhaps a little conversation might be useful so I said "Is he hurt doctor?" well he said "Hurt, man, hurt, why look at that pullover". After that, of course I thought in the army you don't have casual conversation with officers even if you do know them very well, so I said nothing more. Well, George wasn't badly hurt, in fact he wasn't hurt at all of course and was able to walk back down the hill with the rest of us, and so that was the morning exercise.

95

A few Sundays after that there was another exercise, this time with the regular army. Now half way between Partridge Green and Cowfold there's Cowfold Monastery. Cowfold Monastery has got a very big farm surrounding it and in the middle of this very big farm is Monastery Wood, it's a real thicket. The exercise this time was that half a dozen regular soldiers were to try and infiltrate through the wood. They were to go in at the north end and were to work their way through trees and bushes and brambles and come out at the south end. The job of the Partridge Green Home Guard was to place themselves all through the wood at various points and they had to try and spot the regulars as they wormed their way through the wood.

We as Home Guard First Aid men were required to be present and so we stood on the southern outskirts of the wood, talking, just waiting, nothing much to do, everything was quietness. That morning we had with us in the first aid a young fellow named Tom, about seventeen very nearly eighteen. He was doing a bit of training with the Home Guard while waiting to be called up and Greenwood had given him one pip, that is he was a 2nd lieutenant, so of course he was over us and so, whilst we didn't call him sir, we knew that he was in a grade above any of us.

We hadn't been there very long when suddenly Tom the woodsman said, "I know this wood very well you know, when the hunt used to meet they used often to come here looking for foxes and a little way into this wood there's a tremendous fox hole in a bank. Let's go and have a look at it shall we?" So as we had nothing else to do we followed Tom along a path and then he pointed out this great fox hole, right in the bank, mind you it was all covered in brambles and bushes and you couldn't really see very far into it.

As we looked at it, suddenly Tom had a brilliant idea, he said "I've got a thunderflash in my pack." Now a thunderflash is a kind of outsized firework which when it is lit and thrown goes off with a resounding bang, and so Tom lit this firework and he threw it into the middle of this clump of brambles, right in the direction of this fox's hole. Ooh it went bang alright, rooks flew out of the trees with tremendous cawing, flapping wings of pigeons everywhere, the birds were all calling, and there was such a bang. But there was also a dreadful cry as well and as the bang reverberated around, a head with a tin hat a black face came up through the brambles, yelling. It was one of the regular soldiers. I think Tom must have thrown this thunderflash nearly on top of him as he was hiding in this fox's hole.

Well, we remembered we were first aid men and so we leapt into the brambles regardless and went towards him saying, "It's alright, it's alright, we're coming, we're first aid men, let's help you, we'll help you out". He looked at us, never have I seen such a look of withering scorn as he directed at us as he said, "You first aid men, you don't think I'll let you lot touch me, do you? No," he said, "I'm alright" and he wouldn't let us touch him, not to see if he was hurt in any way.

Well I don't know what happened after that, whether Tom got hauled over the coals, because of course what he had done was something very, very irregular. I regret to tell you from the Partridge Green Home Guard's point of view, the other five soldiers all worked their way through that wood and the Home Guard never got a sight of any of them. There was only us, first aid men who weren't supposed to go fighting anyway who had flushed out this one regular soldier who was really aggrieved that we had broken the rules and that he too hadn't able to get through the bushes unseen.

We did lots of other things of course. For instance there were times that we had to do guard duty at night. We'd go on duty about 10 o'clock and in our hut there were a number of camp beds and we would lie down and perhaps sleep till midnight or two o'clock and then we would get up and do a two hour walk around Partridge Green.

On other occasions we used to muster. The fellow who lived farthest away from Partridge Green a distance of 3 miles or 4 miles I suppose at Dial Post, he'd got a telephone. When the call for muster came the people with telephones were notified and they made their way towards Partridge Green knocking up various other fellows all along the way and this was all organised really very well. Somebody used to wake up Teddy Priston and he would come along and he would throw some stones up at my window and I would get up quickly and dress, and we'd all make our way to the yard behind the Railway Hotel. (*Now the Partridge - Ed*)

It all had to be done to see how quickly we could do it. Of course, few of us had cars in those days and those who did hadn't got any spare petrol, so everybody came on a bicycle or on foot and there were some amazing sights. There were some people who came without any teeth, I'd never realised so many Home Guards hadn't got any teeth. Others with their trousers on the wrong way, some without their leggings, most of them had forgotten to put their leather belts on, and quite a few without any hats.

I remember one night when we were all there in record time, Greenwood said "now you Teddy Priston you go out and tell the Colonel that we're mustered". So off went Teddy on his bike, some two miles to where the Colonel lived and he went and hammered on the door, the front door, the Colonel put his head out of the bedroom window just over with a nightcap on and said "Yes, who's that?" "Oh, we be all mustered sir" " Oh yes" said the Colonel "I remember, go and tell them to go back to bed" and so Teddy turned back with the message. That was mustering, we did that on several occasions.

The time came of course when the great number of troops around Partridge Green all moved out and a great number of Canadians moved in. It was then that there was a gas scare and so the Home Guards were required to know something about gas, and so I remember Vic Greenwood said "I want you to come with me, to Billingshurst where a Canadian officer is lecturing about gas, how to deal with it and what to do." Greenwood asked me to take notes of the lecture and on the Thursday night give the lecture to the Partridge Green Home Guards, then the week after to the Cowfold Home Guard, and so I did this.

Then a few Sundays after that Greenwood said that all the Home Guards were to go down to Steyning to the rifle range; there was a huge rifle range there at the foot of the Downs, with great targets set in the chalk on the side of the Downs. All the Home Guards used to go on Sundays for practice but I wasn't to go for that, I was to go with other NCOs from the various platoons to learn something about being in a gas filled room.

Well they'd built a gas proof room there and so we gathered with a man from the regular army and other NCOs and went into this little room. It was built in the middle of a field and had windows all round with an airtight door. We went in and stood in a circle. We put our respirators on and in the centre of this room there was a canister of gas. This was turned on by the regular soldier, all the doors were shut tight — we were to know what it is like to be in a gas filled room — and so clouds of gas enveloped us.

Now that Sunday morning the Canadians had been having manoeuvres on the Downs and they'd been firing with live ammunition and a couple of shells had fallen in Steyning. One fellow had been hurt and there had been some damage to property, but we didn't know anything about that at the time.

We were in this room, all facing to centre and surrounded by this thick gas, when suddenly there was an almighty bang, all the windows came in, or perhaps they went out, and the door burst open and we were all thrown to the ground. For myself it was like being kicked in the middle of my back by a cart horse. We were on the ground, there in the midst of all this smoke and gas, respirators on. We quickly picked ourselves up of course. Then I realised as the gas began to clear through the open windows and door, that the man standing next to me had received a burst of shrapnel, right in the middle of his chest. Oh, it was a terrible sight, but again, we remembered we were first aid men and we picked him up as gently as we could and we carried him through the open door and we laid him down on a blanket and I got a bandage which we always carried and I placed it on this gaping hole in his chest.

97

I remember I was fascinated as I watched what I'd been taught about the effects or the results of shock, the pallor, the slow breathing and so on. It was all taking place in front of my very eyes there as this man lay on the ground in agony. This was only for a minute or two of course as an ambulance came tearing up and officers in cars, and we were told to run, to run for our lives which needed no saying and we made off out of this field towards the place where the army lorries had brought us that morning. It was an amazing sight, I'd never seen anything like it, all these khaki clad figures, hundreds of them, running for their lives across this open countryside from the foot of the Downs.

Well, the man died and later on in the week I was one of those who went to his funeral. He belonged to the Nuthurst Home Guard. We didn't really know what had happened until years later. The Canadians with a tank, they were going up and down the Downs in what is called the Steyning Bowl, a kind of fold in the hills, very, very steep. (It's the place where nowadays they do hangliding). The tanks were there and they were coming up and firing as they came. Some of the shells didn't go along the Downs as intended. One landed right on, or at least beside, the gas proof hut.

Soon after that the Canadians all went and of course D Day came and the pressure was not on the Home Guard as it had been. The summer that the war ended, when we got through to about Whitsuntide I think it was, and Greenwood announced that he thought it was time that we had a little relaxation and everybody welcomed this. We of course had not been able to go down to the sea at Shoreham for two or three years, the coast road and all the coast was banned. There were very few things of an entertaining nature on any of the Bank Holidays or anything like that. He said, "We're going to have a demonstration".

I can't remember if it was Whit Sunday or August Bank Holiday, and he said, "I will organise a demonstration. We'll have a mock battle of the Home Guard all day, and let off some thunderflashes and various other yelling about in the park". It was to be held in the cricket field; in those days it was the park, a huge open space adjoining Partridge Green where the cricket pavilion was with lots of oak trees, and just the right situation for a demonstration of this kind. He said, "The fire brigade can squirt some water about, you first aid people can carry a casualty or two and we will get the ARP to rescue somebody from a blazing building or something like that and we can entertain the Partridge Green people. Oh, I'll tell you what else we could do — we'll have a 5th Columnist".

Now of course we'd all been hearing a lot about 5th Columnists, in the countries of Belgium and France and Holland, then there were the people behind the German lines disrupting communications and things like that. And so he asked for volunteers, somebody who would be a 5th Columnist. The volunteer, unknown to us of course at the time, was Basil Sayers. Now Basil was the local village draper, a man in his fifties, and Basil was going to be the 5th Columnist.

From where I live here at Jolesfield, just up the road, about two fields up, there used to be a rag and bone business and it was run by a couple of brothers whom we all knew as Tom and Steve. Steve was the older and was getting on for 70 and so was too old for the Home Guard, but Tom, he was a member. They had a most amazing place, they'd got about a 2 acre field, they would go around the village collecting rags, bones, anything that was going that people wanted to get rid of. Their yard was full of galvanised baths, they even had a traction engine up there, old motor cars, pipes, all kinds of junk. You could go up there and you could buy almost anything you wanted. And of course they had lots of animals.

They had half a dozen old horses, dogs, cats by the dozen, tame rabbits, a donkey, lots of goats as well as a billygoat — my, when the wind was in the north did we get a smell of billygoat. These all lived together; the couple, Tom and Steve, they slept in an old roadman's caravan and they had built a wooden hut, a big wooden hut, and if you went up to see them, you never knew where to go quite, but you'd probably find them both in the wooden hut where they'd got a fireplace and where they had their meals and most likely there'd be a donkey looking over the double door into the room where they were. You'd shout "Tom, Steve can you come out?" as there wasn't any door to knock at, and they would look round for what you wanted.

Steve used to go into the village every day and so did Tom. They always wore clogs, and Steve was quite a character. He used to go along the road in these clogs pushing a perambulator and he wore what must have been a very good quality black suit, but now it was almost completely green. The trousers were cobbled together at the knees by binder twine, the swallow tail coat, that was as green as could be, and on his head he wore what had once been a beautiful homburg hat, but Steve had pushed the crown up into the air, and I used to think he looked like Robinson Crusoe.

So you'd see Steve go down the road every morning pushing this perambulator and tied onto the spring of the perambulator would be Steve's dog. He would collect round the village, rags, bones, rabbit skins, old tins, anything, what was left over from Jumble Sales; he'd come back up the road in the afternoon and load it up scarcely able to get back to his hut.

Basil went along to see Steve and he borrowed all that lot. He borrowed the clothes, went without shaving for a week because Steve never shaved more often than once a week, and he got some brown paint, because Steve used to sweep chimneys sometimes, so his complexion wasn't exactly pale. Basil borrowed the heavy clogs, and the black suit and the perambulator complete with rags and bones. The only thing he didn't have was the dog as the dog wouldn't go with him. So he set off on this Monday. We of course had marched through the village to the sound of the martial music — all people looking out their windows thought 'my, don't they look a fine lot of men' well, that's what we hoped anyway.

Presently, towards the middle of the afternoon they were amazed to see what they thought was Steve, pushing his perambulator through the High Street. Steve had got rheumatism and this meant that he'd got a particular kind of gait, a hobble, and Basil had caught this to perfection. The old ladies who hadn't gone to the demonstration and were watching out of their windows they thought, 'goodness, there's old Steve, he can't even have a day off on a Bank Holiday, he's out to see what he can get'. Basil went slowly through the High Street and he chose his moment well; he didn't go in the first gateway, the main gateway into the park, he went along to the back entrance and there he went into the back entrance to the park. The moment he chose was when the battle was going on between the Home Guards, there were bangs and shooting and yellings and so on. A couple of really respected Home Guards had been put in charge of the dustbins at the back of the cricket field, because there under one dustbin, Greenwood had hidden a big sheet of paper tied up with red ribbon. The two Home Guards were told to keep their eyes on it because this was what the 5th Columnist was going to come and try and get hold of.

When the battle was going on, for a moment or two they'd taken their eyes off the dustbins and had gone round to the front of the pavilion. This was just what Basil wanted. And so quite leisurely he pushed the pram across the field and up to the dustbins, took the lid off one, extracted a bottle, put the lid back went on to the next one, took out a few tins and put them in amongst the other bones and things in the pram, then looking round, not a soul in sight, turned over the dustbin, picked up the papers that were hidden there and stuffed them in the perambulator along with all the rest of the stuff, turned and equally leisurely made his way back across the field and out into the road.

When he got clear of the park of course he quickened his steps and the same old ladies looking out their windows were amazed to see what they thought was Steve almost running with the perambulator, weaving from side to side, in Basil's efforts to get clear before anyone spotted anything about him. Well he went back and deposited the pram back with Tom and Steve, got on his bike and came back to the field, oh and he took Steve's clothes off, and the great heavy boots, and changed into his Home Guard uniform.

The proceedings were drawing to a close in the cricket field, Greenwood was making a speech and he was hoping everybody had enjoyed themselves and so on, and he was saying "There's just one more thing. There's been a 5th Columnist around today and we think he was after some papers which we have got hidden underneath one of the dustbins at the back of the pavilion. I want the two Home Guards who have been keeping guard to come forward". Naturally they were two of our sergeants, one had got a stiff leg and the other one, well, he was quite elderly, and so they came forward. Greenwood said "Well, sergeants, have you seen anybody?" "No sir, there bain't been nobody round here, no, nobody's come." "Are you quite sure?" "Oh yes sir, we watched the dustbins all the time" and then he said, "Well, go and get the papers then".

Well everybody expected the sergeants to come back with the papers and of course they looked under the dustbin and they were gone. They came back with long faces, "They bain't there sir, they be gone". "Oh dear" said Greenwood, "that means the 5th Columnist has got them, oh dear". That was the moment for Basil to come forward waving the papers in triumph. He was a great fellow Basil and it made a very good ending to what had been a most enjoyable day.

Really, that's almost the end of the talk on Dad's Army, with all the adventures we had, all the fellowship, all the enjoyment, just one other thing.

There was an airstrip about four or five miles away toward the next village of Henfield and there again we used to have to guard through the night, and it was there that I learnt that how even one stripe is something in the army. We arrived, the Partridge Green Home Guard, in an army lorry and the officer came forward and he said to me, "Corporal, it will be your job to see to the tea", "Certainly sir,". He said "I'll detail a man to help you". Well, I thought, that's alright, until this man who knew a lot more about how they made tea than I did, produced a gas cylinder and lit it and on it he put a huge billycan full of water which began to heat up. The officer had entrusted to my care a huge tin containing tea and sugar and powdered milk. I opened the tin, when the water was boiling I tipped it in, that was all I had to do really. Except when it had boiled for a few minutes I called the men, and they all came along with their mugs and I dipped a cup into this mixture and gave a cupful to each man. When they'd all had their cup of tea I had a cup for myself. My goodness, never have I tasted such dreadful witches brew, I don't like powdered milk anyway, but this was strong, oh it was terrible.

Having completed what was my job to make the tea, my helper threw out what was left and went and washed up the billycan and turned out the gas. I said "When is it my turn to do guard duty?" and was told, "Oh, you're the corporal, you don't have to do any guard duty, you can go to bed now". And so I did, I lay down on the bed and slept peacefully throughout the night.

When I did the talk there were usually questions. One of the questions that had been asked a time or two was "Do you think the Home Guard were any good?" and I have two answers to that. The first answer is that I'm completely sure that a great many elderly people slept much sounder in their beds because something like a million men up and down the counties of Britain were keeping guard and were trained in some way at any rate to defend them.

The second thing is that I don't think Hitler ever knew quite what to make of the British Home Guard. When he was making his plans for invasion in the earlier days of the war, he could never leave out of the count the fact that there were these million men who were Home Guards and were there to defend the country.

I'm very pleased that I was one of them, not ashamed.

The Auxiliary Fire Service

By Colin Rudling

The Fire Station was situated at the northern end of "The Partridge", which was then called The Station Hotel, in Church Road. As the name implies all the men were volunteers. Four firemen manned the post at night times, sleeping in makeshift bunks at the station.

A large bell hung by the door that the public could use to raise the alarm. There was also a telephone to contact the exchange in the village post office from where other services could be alerted. The Fire Station was equipped with a trailer pump (see picture below) and a Bedford Fire tender.

Partridge Green Auxiliary Fire Crew
Left to Right

| Bob Packham | Albie Jones | George Simmons | Rex Trot | Jack Hemsley | Bert Fielder | Bob Tidey | Bill Lyle | Charlie Yeo |

The most momentous events they had to deal with were the V1 Flying Bomb (see p129 and p18), and the crashed Ju 88 Bomber (see p133 and p17). The crew was highly praised for its speedy response and efficiency on both occasions.

There was also an A.F.S. at Dial Post with a fire station near to the bus garage. They were equipped with a trailer pump and had twice weekly fire drills. There was a roster of four men on duty each night - just enough to operate the pump. The pump is shown on the right with Bob Greenfield. As far as we know their services were not needed in Dial Post but they were occasionally on stand-by duty in Horsham.

The full crew is pictured on the next page.

Dial Post Auxiliary Fire Service Crew

Back row: (Left to right) Ken Edmonds, Jim Agate, Bert Twine, Frank Longhurst, George Woods, Fred Turrell, Bill Longhurst, Stan Humber, Frank Knight, Mr Edmonds.
Front Row: (Left to right) Lou Short, Bill Weaver, Jack Mills, Bert Allen, Bob Greenfield, Arthur Deare, Fred Lucas, Roy Short.

Ken Edmonds (extreme left back row) joined Dial Post Auxiliary Fire Service around 1944 at the age of eighteen. He lived with his parents at Rook Cross Farm, and his father was also in the AFS. Ken is believed to be the only surviving member of the Dial Post AFS.

Members of the Fire Guard parading, probably on VE Day, in Partridge Green High Street

Dial Post during World War Two

By Derek Saunders

Dial Post did not have any major incidents during WW2, however it was an important place for a few reasons. I am extremely fortunate that the following kind and wonderful people were good enough to allow me to record and write down their memories. I've decided that for the most part I can do no better than **'to write it as they told it'**.

Den Field with May and Tony Warnett

Ada Giles

Bette Sawyer

When War Broke Out Tony was 13, May was 9 and Den 14. Bette was 16. Ada was to become an evacuee.

"I am speaking to you from the Cabinet Room at 10 Downing Street. This morning the British Ambassador in Berlin handed the German Government a final note stating that, unless we hear from them by 11 o'clock that they were prepared at once to withdraw their troops from Poland, a state of war would exist between us. I have to tell you now that no such undertaking has been received, and that consequently this country is at war with Germany."

Tony, May and Den were on top of the horse and wagon during haymaking. It was just after 11 o'clock on 3rd September 1939. Harry Grover who owned the garage came and told us that Mr Chamberlain had said war was declared. May also says "I have a vivid memory in June 1940 I was up the school, lunch time I suppose, I met Mr. Clarke the postman and he said France had fallen. It did not mean much to me. He was so upset so serious you know that they had captured France on our doorstep".

Home Guard

Den: My father organized the Home Guard and the Fire service to start with. Then Mr George Daniels was in charge with around 30 members, the numbers changed all the time. I was an ARP messenger first then went into the Home Guard later on. The meetings were held up at The

Guest House next to Blaker's, which is now a private house. All our ammunition and all that sort of thing used to be in the big lockup pantry there. Earlier on it was up on the Ashurst Road, there used to be a hut up there in Honeybridge Lane, it was a high point where there was a telephone mast there, but we never used it. They did when it was up there. We had two different sorts of rifles, we had a mortar, and we had an automatic rifle and a sten gun and we kept them at home. We used to go on our bikes to Home Guard lectures at Henfield and to Steyning rifle range. We used to be on manoeuvres down at Bay Bridge and the Canadians used to fire live ammunition over our heads. I will never forget that. Sometimes we had Mr Allen's lorry from The Crown, he used to help Dial Post out.

Tony: Dad was in it from the beginning and in 1941 he got National Service and when he came out from there they were collecting up building workers bricklayers, plumbers, anybody in the building trade. I assume it was for over military age about 60. Then they sent them away to the old aerodromes in the West Country. Dad got sent down to Cirencester around that area with a local lad he worked with. They all went and that left me at home doing all the veg and the gardening.

May: When they started they had nothing only a stick. But, let's face it; it was soon very well organized. You all got these instructions and you didn't question a thing. Today you would think why I have to do these things.

Ada: Later on when people got to know me and found that I was good at needlework I became more accepted, and when the Home Guard eventually got dropped off a load of uniforms they brought them to me to shorten arms and legs and take in waists etc. That was good for me too because they used to give me a couple of bob and often a rabbit as well. We loved rabbit stew.

'The Brave Boys of Dial Post.' Outside the garage at Buck Barn.
From left to right:- Unknown,Bob Luckings, 'Jock'Martin; Lt.Daniels; Ern Sparkes; Unknown; Bill Ellicker; Ron Martin; Arthur Flint; George Woods; Jack Bean; TEd Woolgar. Photograph courtesy of Ron Martin, related also that Ern Sparkes died on an exercise.

Air raids

Den: We had a telephone and my father was an air raid warden and if he was at home when there was an air raid he would sound a klaxon and when it was over he would blow a whistle. You could hear the siren from Horsham. In the beginning it was fresh to every body and they did

104

not know the exact procedure, but we soon got into a routine over it all. Our house was full of gas masks. The one you had to put on the baby was a big one and you had to pump it up. Even in 1938 my dad could see it coming and had the blackout curtains made up. We all had blackout materials and ways of doing things. It was pitch black outside you couldn't see anything. Yes you wouldn't dare show a light. Not that we had a car at that time but some people did. If you went up the pub at night it was completely blacked out.

May: My grandmother got fed up as she had the same whistle for her dogs you see. My mother said she would never put her gas mask on so I thought "oh dear, she will be gone too". If you went outside you had to put your light out first in case there was an airplane up there. Poor animals, I was terrified about my cat.

Tony: Before it all started we were all issued with gas masks. I think the first term we went back to school we had to carry our gas masks in a box with a piece of string.

Bette: High explosive bombs and incendiary devices were dropped north of our farm one night, with one high explosive bomb falling behind a thicket opposite Medlars Cottage in Swallows Lane, well the next morning we went to explore the hole only to find a great mound of earth, the bomb had gone down in the ground and had not exploded and to this day I do not remember it being retrieved. I think it must still be there in the ground. Others that were dropped nearby all exploded. Oil bombs were dropped near our farm.

May: At school we had airmen from the New Zealand air force who were based at the airfield in Coolham come and give us a lecture on New Zealand, it was very interesting.
We had a brick wall built outside the cloakroom door. Now this cloakroom had a galvanized roof. They built this big bomb blast wall and every time there was a raid you heard the klaxon and we had to go into the cloak room you see because we had got the blast wall.   Before that we had to get under the desk. In my case by the time I had got my glasses off and got my gas mask on I was always last. I do not know why we had to put our gas masks on as there wasn't any gas. I was always last but that was before they built the bomb blast wall. We would have stayed under our desks wouldn't we; I think they did that in all schools. They left it there for years. I do not know when they took that down.

Tony: The school attendance when we left in the August holiday of 1939 was 28 and it was 65 when we went back, cos of the evacuees you see.

Lifestyle Changes

Tony: All the railings of what they call the Pen they took all of that lot. All metal stuff, they took all the junk down to the corner where the telephone box was. Fetes and things were arranged to collect money to buy Spitfires and things. In the shop we had a gauge showing how much we got and what was coming and I think we bought a submarine. You could not buy things any more. You had to make and mend.

May: If you had dividing railings, they did not take those but anything else outside the house they went, gates and everything. We had this dump beside the telephone box which was down by the Granary, it has got the balcony by the telephone box, everybody put their aluminium there, old saucepans and anything metal and they came and it was collected. In those days you didn't throw saucepans away you mended them with round metal things.
All the road numbers were taken down and the names, in case there were spies. Especially in the village if you didn't know somebody you would assume they were spies. The Land Army occupied the top floor of Dial Post House. The rest of the house continued as before because it was a farm. Some of the Land Army girls worked at Dial Post Farm. You did what you were told during the war. That was it, nobody questioned it.

Den: The band and the football club had to pack up because all the boys went. I was just getting to the age to be going into the football team.

Tony: Well there wasn't much chance to do anything after working on the farm day and night. You used to have to work in the garden as well.

Den: Then there was overtime for the harvesting etc, and in between that I was doing training in Horsham but it was full time and we never had time off, it was seven days a week.

Tony: At the end Den would probably have Saturday afternoon off and then he would go in Sunday afternoon. And I would have Sunday afternoon off. And that was after they said you had to have one half day a week wasn't it? I suppose it did not apply to us farmers who only had a few cows and pasture land and then we were told you had to have one afternoon off. Some people's vehicles got commandeered for the war effort but there wasn't many that had a vehicle in Dial Post. Mr Allen from the Crown retained his lorry. He had to go to London to take bricks up and he used to come back to Ashington with cattle food and rubble, he got special fuel allowance for that. He was a bit of a workaholic. Even in the blitz he was going up there with the lorry.

Bette Sawyer, (née Lucking), moved into Swallows farm in 1928 when she was 4 and went to school in Dial Post. Bette was 16 when war broke out and worked on the farm 7 days a week during the war, and all her working life.

Bette: I was very disappointed that I was not allowed to join the Land Army as I was already an agricultural worker. I was also annoyed that I had to use my clothing coupons for replacement working clothes whereas the Land Army girls got theirs issued and replaced as needed, however my friends in the Land Army would pass on their clothes to me when they got replacements. The Land Army girls used to work on my father's farm during harvesting time. Male agricultural workers did not join the forces unless they chose to do so.
I always wanted to be an actress and I got a group of people together, (some from the Home Guard and some from the Fire Watch), and we would rehearse at our farm or another members house and then we put on several concerts at Dial Post village hall in aid of the Red Cross. We also did concerts at Steyning and Ashington; we raised quite a lot of money for the war effort. My father would take us to the venues in his car, "whilst he was on his way to the vet etc"; as it was illegal to make a journey in a vehicle unless it was work related or necessary. We used to have paraffin delivered by a tanker and on one occasion it got stuck in our back track and the driver, whilst waiting for help, took his banjo out and started playing it so he got roped in to do a turn at the concerts along with a soldier who used to sing while his wife played the piano.
Iron railings went from around the shop, everything went except where it separated properties.

Den: Charlie Holdstock the policeman from Partridge Green was like a second father to all the children, he used to like homemade wine particularly and he used to come round our house, "to check the dog licence", and he would always sit down and have a glass or two of mum's homemade wine, he used to like mums parsnip wine. He visited several houses when he came to Dial Post and he was very merry and then he had to ride his bike back to Partridge Green. On some Saturday evenings he would stand outside the telephone box by the old granary, (he would keep away from any trouble from the Canadian forces at the village hall), waiting for his sergeant to phone and he would have a pint of beer but someone would have to get it for him from the Crown and someone else would have to hold it for him in case his chief came along.

Den: Dial Post Fire Service was very active, one day they pumped out a well for practice and another day for practice they pumped out the spring outside our house.

Food

Tony: There were chickens and rabbits. We all lived on rabbits. We had plenty of chickens. We had some big army biscuits in the cellars at Charley Bentley's at New Lodge Farm. We were not starving like they were in Holland.

May: You know you see pheasants on the side of the road? Dad would bring one home. Nothing wrong with them. I couldn't eat anything like that now. No we never went hungry did we. At haymaking we got double rations. My mother had all the butter and sugar for cooking and there was never any left for tea, I've never gone back to it. Talking about rations, we had some emergency rations above the shop and there was a big can of army biscuits sealed but they did go out of date sometimes so they opened them up and we used to have them at school and paid a half penny for them and had them at break and they were good.

Bette: Everyone grew their own food. Father used to kill a pig every year and they would salt it or hang it up the chimney to smoke though it was a bit tough after a while. We had chickens and kept bees, we used to get an extra ration of sugar for the bees in the winter.

Ada: Sometimes they would get extras up at the shop and they would always make sure every family had some. My George would always bring me plenty of cigarettes when he came home on leave; they were given them in the forces.

Casualties

Den: An English airman parachuted from a plane and hit an oak tree near Sunte and unfortunately was killed.
Bette: One evening we saw an airplane come over on fire and it came down in a field near Broomers Corner. We got on our bicycles and rode over there, (goodness knows what for), and we scrambled through a hedge to get as close as possible, (and I bumped into a lump of metal which we discovered in the morning was a bomb), it was a Junkers. Unfortunately the crew of 4 were killed.
One day a large number of German aircraft were heading for London during the blitz. We were in a field haymaking, and one aircraft came low above us and we were told to run through the hedge, which we did and we got stung and scratched because we were wearing sleeveless tops. That was really frightening.

Canadian Forces

Tony: We had the Bow Bells first they were the London Division. Then we had three divisions of Canadians. First, second and third. The Canadian forces were in residence at Knepp Castle. The Burrells moved to Floodgates.

Den: The Canadian hospital was in Ashington, and the headquarters for their Dental Corps was in The Guest House here in Dial Post, they used to perform dental operations there. They had an armed guard outside as this was also the headquarters of our Home Guard.

Bette: The Canadian forces would attend the dances at the village hall every Saturday night and every other Thursday and very often they used to end up having fights amongst themselves and their MPs would come and take them away, also they used to stick chewing gum under the chairs. My dad used to walk with me to and from the dances and he would wait at the Crown and collect me at 10:30.
The 1st Division of Canadian forces had been prisoners in Canada and were freed providing they agreed to go into the forces overseas, but they were still trouble. They broke into the wine cellar at Knepp and drank all the wine.
They were on manoeuvres around our farm, (Swallows), and due to one of them throwing a hand grenade in the wrong place it exploded and caught our bean rick on fire and that then spread to the hay rick next to it and both burnt to the ground which meant all my dad's animal feed for the year was gone. Sir Merrik Burrell came over and was very concerned that he had lost all his animal feed and he advised dad that he was to "go and see my man and take whatever you need." Sir Merrik Burrell didn't like the Canadians because they used to shoot his ducks on the lake. The general's driver used to swim out and get them.
The Canadians always asked for spirits at the Crown and Mr Allen said he didn't have any but there was always some available for some special residents, like Mr Pacey, who had the shop, when he went in after he closed up the shop for the day, there was always some for him; he used to hide it behind the curtains in case the Canadians came in.

In the first week of June 1944 a convoy of vehicles left Knepp Castle and a despatch rider asked my mum if he could stay overnight to say his goodbyes and he explained that he could catch up the convoy in the morning. Mum said he could.

Ada: Joyce Field married a Canadian and so did Tribitha (Bycee) Sparkes, but she was disappointed to find it wasn't as she had been told and came back after two years.

American Forces

Tony: The Americans practised for the D-Day glider landings and take offs near Sunte and at Knepp (for taking the equipment to France). In the fields they put all these iron posts in with cables so that planes couldn't land because the wires would trip them all up. The 12 acre field across from Bentons Farm, what used to be old Pink Cottage farm, they never did it there, we could never make out why they never done it in there. Then we saw they left it alone for the Lysanders to land the army spotter planes. They used to try and land there like. For it was all practice for them you see. The British and the Americans used it. They had all army telephones down there; they would use it for manoeuvres. They were allowed to drive vehicles straight through and park there. They used to do what they liked. I remember barrage balloons used to come loose and they used to come up dragging cables, when they come down low someone would try to secure it to a field gate. One came down at Ashington and lifted the gate off its hinges. For the invasion you heard them going through Dial Post. Tanks going through in the middle of the night. If you were on your bicycle you had to get out of the way. All along the South Coast the hotels were made over for the military and we were a second line of defence. We couldn't go there.

Den: They came in with Dakotas which would drop down low and raise the smaller gliders, a pole came up and a little while later you would see the plane with the glider. They couldn't do that with bigger ones as their load was bigger and heavier. They broke them up and took it by road, some of them had a jeep inside them.

May: We were not supposed to know what was going on were we? I kept thinking where I could go. In the woods with my tabby cat? And then I thought the tanks would go in the woods, and the lorries, and I did not know where to go with my cat. I was in such a state.

Evacuees

Tony: My cousins from Lewisham and their dog came down and stayed with us but they went back after about a year because they were missing out on their education. Their knowledge was far more advanced than us down here. Unfortunately one of them was killed when a bomb landed on their school; the other one had left by that time. We had my cousin Ray's dog throughout the war.

May: If you had two bedrooms and you was husband and wife then you had to have evacuees. The WVS took them round; they would know who had a spare bedroom. I always remember my mother said one little boy she took to Butchers Row and being a London boy he said "Where are the door bells or knockers". My mum said in the country you banged on the door with your fist, and he couldn't understand that as in London they all had knockers or bells. There were 6 of us; I was sleeping in the kitchen at one time. They were bored as they missed their cinemas.

Ada: I remember a lot of evacuees staying at Glebe house in West Grinstead. All the others went back to London after the war. Village people used to 'give me the elbow as they didn't like townies', to start with at least.

Ada Giles lived in Mitcham, her husband George was in the navy, and in 1940, (due to the bombings) Ada came to live with her sister-in-law at Wharf cottage in West Grinstead. A friend of Ada's, (Mrs Stone), who also lived in Mitcham found out where Ada was living and came down with her 10 year old daughter, knocked on their door and asked if there was anywhere they could find board and lodgings. Fortunately Mrs Brocker opposite took them in. A short while later a Mr Weaver advised Mrs Brocker that he had an empty cottage in Dial Post. Mrs Short rented it and took in Ada and her young son Barry, to help pay the rent; this was two houses away from the village hall (Glenavon). They got on very well together, but of course, Ada wanted a place of her own. In 1942 Ada went to the council offices in Storrington with her friend Mrs Stone and they both filled in council house application forms. Two weeks later Mrs Stone received a letter with a key for a council house in Ashington. Ada never heard a thing. Ada offered to take over the rent for the house in Dial Post but Mr Weaver decided he wanted his house back and said to Ada, "whilst I can't put you out, I would like you to go". A few days later Ada was walking her children down Bentons Lane and bumped into Annie Warnett who advised her that the "Butler" family in the old bungalow, (Beehive), wanted to move out. Ada asked Mr Sparkes who owned Beehive if she could rent the bungalow if Mr Weaver would take on the Butler family as tenants. This was agreeable to everyone and Ada and her children moved into Beehive in Bentons Lane.

P.O.W.s

Den: We had Germans working with us at Bentons Farm. They cleared out all the rivers. You know where you go to the Bentons Place where the river goes under the lane; well the Italians were cleaning all that out. They used to have an army guard who had a rifle and a ganger who told them what they had to do. And I with my own eyes, I have seen a prisoner holding the rifle while the guard got up the bank and then hand it back to him. They used to have their macaroni on a pole.

Bette: They were brought over from Billingshurst, but some stayed at Shipley. They came to work on the farms, they brought their rations with them but mother used to make them a cup of tea. It was Italians at first, we did not have the Germans till later on; they would not let them out. They were pleased not to have been sent to the Russian Front. They were just ordinary people like us. They did not want to start the war. We had one working on our farm, (Swallows), and he saw a piece of furniture, a roll top desk which was in a state. He didn't speak much English but he explained he wished to refurbish it for us, which he did. He made a beautiful job of it and then polished it, we have still got it. This particular German POW explained to us that he was a farmer in Germany and was so upset with the German forces when they took all his farm horses.

May: They were happy fellows, the Italians. They used to sing opera all the time.

The Military Presence in This Area

By Colin Rudling

At the outbreak of war large numbers of Canadian troops arrived in England to help defend us against the very real threat of a German invasion. Once the threat of invasion was over most of the troops went on to fight in Europe, on or soon after D Day.

Many of the troops were billeted in large country houses. In our area Knepp Castle, West Grinstead Park, Clock House, Shermanbury Place and Shermanbury Grange were all used for this purpose, and this pattern was repeated all over South East England.

There was also a British Army searchlight unit based in a field just north of the Windmill pub at Littleworth. It did not have an anti aircraft battery; its purpose was to lock its beam onto German bombers so that our nightfighters could shoot them down. The unit did have a heavy machine gun for defence, which I believe was used a few times. I imagine it was a popular posting for the soldiers who apparently spent most afternoons in the pub.

Knepp Castle was the forward headquarters of the 1st. Canadian Division and its General was in charge of all troops in this area, including British. As well as Headquarters and signals staff there was a detachment of fifty Lorne Scots of the Canadian Army to act as body guard for the General. These guards slept in the stable block at Knepp Castle.

Signalman Ed Gauthrean 3rd Canadian Signals Division, on West lawn of Shermanbury Grange

On the 9th. March 1944 King George VI visited the Division "A" Mess HQ at West Grinstead Lodge in Park Lane. The Lodge was demolished in the 1970's.

On the same day the King also visited the 2nd. Canadian Infantry Division at Billingshurst.

Left: King George VI (Courtesy of Keystone)

West Grinstead Lodge prior to World War 2 (Courtesy of John Winstanley)

Considerable damage was caused by troops on manoeuvres, having to drive large vehicles on our narrow country roads often in blackout conditions. Numerous fences, gates etc were crashed into, as was the gents toilet at the Burrell Arms. Claims for the cost of repairs were met by the military authorities.

Not all the damage however was accidental. Before handing over Knepp Castle to the Canadians and moving to Floodgates Farm the owners, Sir Merrik and the Hon. Mrs Burrell, took the precaution of bricking off the entrance to the wine cellar. This proved to have been in vain, as the following report, printed in the Sussex Daily News on 5th June 1942 illustrates:

"The discovery that a grating and iron bars had been torn away from the vent of the bricked-in cellar of Knepp Castle, and wine stolen to the value of £306, led to the appearance of three Canadian soldiers at Horsham yesterday. They were committed for trial.

Sergeant John Joseph Gunn, Corporal Frederick Thomas Simpson, and Private Leonard Roy were charged with stealing 41 magnums and 143 bottles of port, the property of Major Walter Burrell and Sir Merrik R Burrell, Bt., C.B.E. The soldiers made statements that they took the wine in an army truck.

Gladys Amy Ginger and her husband, Frank Arnold Ginger, of High Street, Nutfield, Surrey, were committed for trial on a charge of receiving the wines. On a further charge relating to six army blankets, boots, anti-gas kit, etc., Mr and Mrs Ginger, for whom Mr. W. Fordham appeared, pleaded not guilty and reserved their defence. They were granted bail.

Sarah Barton (23), married, of Monson Road, Redhill, pleaded not guilty to receiving nine bottles of wine from Sergeant Gunn. She said that on 13th May Gunn, whom she had known for over a year, called at her house in a taxi with the wine, which he took to a wardrobe explaining that it was for a party. 'I did not know the wine was stolen. When I asked him where he got it from he just laughed.'

Mrs. Barton pleaded guilty to a further charge of detaining three blankets, identified as W.D. property, and said that Sergeant Gunn had brought them for her black-out. Superintendent Heritage said that nothing was known against her. When bound over for one year and ordered to pay 19 shillings costs, she broke into tears.

Stewart Ritchie and Hugh David Priddle, two more Canadian soldiers, admitted stealing nine bottles of wine worth £11 5s from Knepp Castle cellar on the 9th May. Both men were given a good character. The Chairman, telling them that the excuse of being in drink did not cut any ice, fined each £3."

Not all the cellar contents were lost however, as a number of bottles of very fine port were found in a nearby pond.

There follows a transcript of a letter sent from the Hon. Mrs Burrell on 21st September 1943 to the Camp Commandant of the 3rd Canadian Division, after they vacated Knepp Castle.

```
Dear Captain Stuart,

     I was sorry that I was unable to see you before you left to check
over the list of things belonging to me which were left out at Knepp
Castle for you. They were:-

1. Double Oak Hanging wardrobe, with chromium plated handles.

2. Blue Wardrobe, last seen in the Quartermaster's stores, Nissen hut.

3. Big brown cupboard with 5 shelves above and 3 drawers and small
cupboard below. Last seen in D&H Orderly Room Hut near rubbish heap.
```

4. House telephone & medicine cupboard in maid's octagonal bedroom.

5. Electric light fittings, bedroom No.5.

6. Electric light chandelier & wall bracket.

7. Electric light lantern outside General's Office.

8. Curtain rods & curtains in Study. Col. Cote's room.

9. Basket grate in hall.

10. Steel grate in parlour.

11. Electric light fittings and 8 cupboards in Gun Room.

12. House telephone, own bedroom (General's Office)

13. 2 electric lanterns, Study passage.

14. 3 grills, 1 hot plate cupboard, marble slab, Aga and Esse implements in kitchen.

15. 1 hot plate cupboard damaged by fire. Table (12 drawers under) serving passage.

16. Implements belonging to boilers & boiler room.

17. Fire escape in top of Tower Room.

18. Two fire hoses, Minimax fire extinguisher & brackets.

19. Various pictures.

I hope that all the above items are present, but have not yet had the opportunity to check these. My Red & White bathroom, (A.D.C.'s Office) and the kitchen and scullery are still locked up.

A few of the things I notice that have happened during your Division's thirteen months occupation are the following:-

1. Parlour chimney & chimney pot split by fire. This happened while papers were being burned recently.

2. Downstairs servant's bathroom: Taps missing, drain blocked.

3. Gate post North Drive and adjoining fence run into and broken.

4. Eyelets for stair-rods on main staircase missing.
                    (Have you got these?)

5. One sun shutter broken off Parlour window.

6. Various oxidised-silver door handles missing, replaced with plastic handles.

7. Various wash-basins broken, including green marble one in bedroom No.5.

8. Oak polished floors wearing badly in many places, particularly in Parlour.

9. Sanitary fittings are more stained.

10. Roof leaked badly over middle staircase and in Tower room.

11. Marble curb-stones & mantelpieces are more damaged than before.

Had you not gone so unexpectedly, I was going to ask you to deal with the following:-

1. Rats over the garage.

2. Creepers and ivy to be cut back from coping stones.

3. Roofs and down spoutings need cleaning.

4. Chimneys need sweeping. (Can you tell me when this was last done?)

   In spite of this formidable list, I should like to thank you and the 3rd Division for distempering most of the house and generally leaving it better and cleaner than you took it over.

        Yours sincerely,
        (The Hon. Mrs. Burrell)

I believe that it was mainly French Canadian troops that were based at West Grinstead Park and Clock House. The 11th Canadian Tank Battalion, Ontario Regiment was at Shermanbury Place.

Shermanbury Grange saw several units come and go, but the one that stayed the longest and had the most impact on the village was the 3rd Royal Canadian Signals Regiment.

Despatch riders of D Company 3rd Canadian Signals,
behind the coal shed at Shermanbury Grange

Left to Right: Signalman William Nelson, Signalman Levesque, Corporal Herb Turvie, Sergeant Cliff Carrothers, Signalman C F Schlievert, Signalman Louis Paternaude, (unknown), Signalman William Gerard, Signalman William Sylvester, (unknown).

In general the soldiers integrated well with the local communities, they put on film shows, held parties for children and for the most part fitted in well with our way of life. In return locals would lay on dances for the troops, invite them into their homes for meals, a tea room was opened in the Methodist Church and of course the pubs were very popular with the soldiers.

Many Canadians met and married local girls some taking their brides back home after the war. Some remained and started new lives over here. Others contributed to the local gene pool in a less conventional manner.

It is probably fair to say that the English speaking Canadians found it much easier to integrate with us than did the French Canadians, who had the language barrier to overcome.

Left to Right
Sergeants Morley Young, Garfield Niven and Charles Norton, 3rd Canadian Signals Division, outside one of the Nissen Huts close to the Partridge Green road at Shermanbury Grange.

Canadian David Wagner of 3rd Canadian Signals, who was based at Shermanbury Grange, on honeymoon with his wife Kay, at "Nortonville" High Street, Partridge Green, home of Mr and Mrs Priddle.

Please let me advise you that I was a member of 3rd Canadian Division Signals (R.C.C.S) stationed at Shermanbury Grange with other members of Headquarters and No 1 Companies during the period August 1942 to September 1943. A further section of No 1 Company, mainly C Section, was stationed at St. Hugh's Charterhouse between the Partridge Green corner and Cowfold.

3 Division H.Q. was at Knepp Castle and as our duties consisted of providing communications from Division H.Q. to other formations of the division, we travelled through Partridge Green to reach Knepp Castle almost on a daily basis. The village therefore became well known to us. It was also well known to us on our off duty hours from the village hall (dances) the several churches, the pubs and rail station. Many of us helped in the off hours on local farms during the 1942 and 1943 harvests. Money earned was immediately turned over to local pub keepers; making for many fond evenings. I recall taking my section on route marches and on motorcycle training to the Cowfold area, so we could drop into the Chalet tea house.

Sergeant Morley Young, pictured between the power house and the Manor House at Shermanbury Grange

I believe that it was at Christmas 1942 the Father Prior of St. Hugh's Charterhouse entertained members of C section at the Chalet. He provided the section with a supper and wine. C section worshipped him.

Proceeding in the other direction we would visit Henfield and the several hotels in that village. I particularly recall "The George". On many occasions we also went to Saturday dances at Henfield.

At the Shermanbury Grange "big house", I recall our nissen huts located to the west of the house, on the Partridge Green side. Our Unit Officer was in the house as were the officers quarters and mess. The main floor also contained the men's main mess hall. The sergeants mess and quarters were in the small house located along the road between the main gate and the Cowfold to Henfield road. We also had several nissen huts close to this house to quarter we sergeants.

I recall the estate agent, a Mr Lewis. He was a fine gentleman. I also recall making a parking area for motorcycles of our dispatch-rider section in the estate coal shed. We cleaned this area and then numbered stalls for the motorcycles D1, D2 etc. with yellow paint. I visited the estate in 1974 and found the numbers still very prominently displayed on the wall.

I recall that the number 17 bus ran from Brighton to Horsham. Most signal members rode that bus many times as it was our main method of transit. Because my Christian name is Morley, I recall Morley Cottage on the road to Cowfold and close to the location of St. Hugh's Monastery.

Many of our unit married while stationed at Partridge Green. I particularly recall that our colonel, Lt. Col. G.O.Gamble, married a local girl. Signalman E Gauthrean married a girl called Iris who came from the Ashington area, Alex Campbell married Hazel from Henfield, Dave Wagner married Kay from Ringmer (picture on previous page), Signalman Sinclair (I don't recall his initials) also married a local girl.

Without doubt your area was, in my opinion, the most beautiful of all those we passed through during our long stay in England,

Sincerely G Morley Young

Parish Council

By Dorothy Banks

It would be difficult to claim, from the evidence of the minutes, that the war had a significant effect on Parish Council business. Although the question of Air Raid Precautions was raised at a parish council meeting in March 1938 and the clerk was instructed to find out from Horsham District Rural Council (HRDC) what the parish council's responsibilities were, they were never mentioned in the records - doubtless for security reasons. Indeed, a few days before war was declared, the council was still apparently engaged wholly in footpaths, stiles and playing fields.

There were thirteen parish councillors, many of them "prominent" people in the parish. Mr Percy Garton had been Chairman for 14 years when he stated that he intended to move away in 1939; he actually stayed on until 1941 because of the effect of the war on the running of Jolesfield school, at which he was headmaster. Other councillors at the outbreak of war were

Albert Burdfield (universally known as Ducky)
Mr J Kidd, who lived at Old Priors
Alfred Medland, farmer at Rooklands
Alfred Pankhurst, of the Tabby Cat at West Grinstead
Stephen Tidey of the Post Office and general stores at West Grinstead
Walter Mitchell, retired butcher, living in Wilton Villa, who died in 1944
Mr R Davis
Cyril Fisher, grocer in Partridge Green at the Post Office
Arthur Pacey, grocer at Dial Post
Mr S W Trigg
Mr Short, farmer at Woodman's in Dial Post
Mrs Green of Caryllhurst, who organised a war canteen near Buck Barn and was so heavily involved in war work generally that she resigned from the council in 1943. She returned as a councillor after the war.

Mr Davis, together with Mr Pacey, who had held the grocers at Pengates since the early 1920s, led a protest by Dial Post residents against the purchase of what became the King George V field in Partridge Green. Dial Post had apparently been trying to get drainage for some 15 years, and felt this would be a better use of money than a playing field. After a public enquiry the purchase went ahead, and administration of the playing field occupied much Parish Council time during the war, as it has done ever since.

Others co-opted during the course of the war as a result of deaths or resignations were Mr Gumbrell, the new headmaster of Jolesfield, Mr A P Lawrence, manager of Forrest Stores, Mr Daniells, Mr Pallant, Mrs Jackson, Herbert Mitchell, the butcher in Partridge Green, and Mr Thornton, farmer of New Barn Farm and a member of the War Agricultural Committee.

Clerk to the Council was Ernest Merritt, who lived at The Andes on the High Street, was by all accounts a very kindly man. His "day job" was as a partner at the butchers, which also involved delivering meat all round the parish. He held the post of clerk for 32 years from 1936 to 1968 when Betty Brown took over.

Ernest and Lilian (née Mitchell) Merritt
Picture courtesy of Henfield Museum

For decades, barely a meeting had passed without some reference to a footpath, bridleway or footbridge in need of repair. Rights of way remained close to the council's heart throughout the war, and there was great indignation when it was discovered that the many paths dug up in the ploughing up campaign had been destroyed without the War Agricultural Committee's permission.

As far as the war effort was concerned, there are brief references to making inventories of iron railings to be scrapped for munitions, lists of wells in the event of mains water being bombed, fund raising efforts (£5,476 was raised in War Weapons Week in 1941), and, eventually in 1944 a War Emergency Committee was formed. But in the main, the council continued to concern itself with more prosaic matters. Nevertheless, most, if not all the councillors were heavily engaged in "war work" in their personal capacity.

Mr Fisher ran the grocery business which operated out of the Post Office in Partridge Green High Street, which in turn was run by Mrs Fisher. According to Doug Pennifold "Mr Fisher spent a lot of effort in fund raising, holding dances, concerts and whist drives in the Village Hall in aid of Spitfire Week, Mrs Churchill's Aid to Russia Fund and many others. The dances were all well attended during the war, with a large number of soldiers there from Shermanbury Grange".

Cyril and Ada Fisher outside the Post Office after the war.   Picture courtesy of John Fisher

Elections were suspended until 1946, but the council continued to meet very much as normal every three months in Jolesfield School, although most of the meetings in 1940 and 1941 were very short. By 1944 talk had moved to post-war planning, especially for the new site for the school and council houses in Partridge Green and Dial Post – councillors were vehemently against the proposed site for houses "north of Burdfield's yard" ie Blanches, but were clearly overruled. Finally, perhaps it was war weariness that caused a suggestion for peace celebrations, after "the subject had been thoroughly discussed" (code for a big fight) to be withdrawn.

Helping the War Effort

By Norman Berry

In the thirties West Grinstead was a reasonably prosperous area — it did not suffer from the hardship and unemployment common in many industrial areas. Although a start had been made to the mechanisation of farming, many of the population were still employed in agriculture. The "Welfare State" was in its infancy and there was a culture of working for various charitable causes, both by collecting funds and by providing material help.

Unemployment was quite high in the Brighton area so regular collections of fruit and vegetables were made for delivery to the needy there. Collections were also made of books, toys and money for the local hospitals. Closer to home the subscription medical services (see the Doctors and Nurses chapter) were not fully self financing, so money was raised to keep them in financial balance. Both local schools, although funded by the Church of England and the State, needed top up funds for keeping the buildings in good repair, etc. These and other similar activities meant that there was a core of people ready and willing to organise local arrangements to assist the War effort.

Early in the war the government introduced "National Savings Certificates" — these were purchased for 15 shillings (75p). The money was loaned to the government for the war effort, and to be paid afterwards. In both Partridge Green and Dial Post collectors would accept 6d (2½p) subscriptions weekly, to build up enough for a certificate. The Bishop of Chichester introduced a "self help" scheme for the local churches, in which members were asked to subscribe money for the church to purchase certificates. When redeemed after the War the money would be used to finance "the many things needed by the church that had been held over during the duration." A similar scheme was instituted for funds for the Village Hall.

Of course the Red Cross was high in the list of priorities for help. Money was raised through the churches and other organisations.

By 1941 the themed weeks for collecting for a particular wartime activity had been introduced. One of the first was the "War Weapons Week" held at Easter. Parish councillor Mr J Kidd was a leading organiser of the events and the following sums were contributed via the local Post Offices for the first:
- West Grinstead (Miss Sendall) - £1,215
- West Grinstead (S.H. Tidey & Co.) - £260
- Dial Post (Mrs. Scard) - £700
- Partridge Green (Mrs. Fisher) - £3,276

A number of social events and sales were used to collect funds.

At this time there was a serious threat of an invasion, so as well as the proposed armed response by the Home Guard and "Secret Army", arrangements were being made for the civilians to cope. The Ministry of Food appointed Voluntary Food Organisers to be responsible for "the equitable distribution of foodstuffs in the event of invasion". Those appointed for the Parish were:
- West Grinstead — Mr. T.C. Gallant of Mid-Sussex Motors Ltd.
- Dial Post — Mr. Bentley of New Lodge Farm.
- Partridge Green — Mr. J. Kidd of Old Priors.

Arrangements were also being made for Dressing Stations for Civilians. In Dial Post, for example, money was being raised to purchase equipment through whist drives, dances and jumble sales. There was also an appeal for a marble-topped washstand, towels, blankets and for sheets to be made into bandages.

In September there was a "National Savings Week" in Partridge Green with the objective of raising £1500 for a searchlight. There was a wide range of events including a Children's Fancy Dress Parade, Dances, Cribbage Drives etc. Decorated prams and cycles were invited for the Children's Fancy Dress Parade but because of the shortage of paper 'natural flowers and foliage' were advised for decoration.

In 1942 fund raising efforts included a "Warship Week" and with Russia in the war Mrs Churchill's "Aid to Russia Fund" was supported. The local Canadian soldiers arranged a concert to raise funds for the "Warship Week". Apparently the highlight was a large hairy soldier who played the part of a fairy. For the "Russia Fund" the local school children were collecting farthings (the farthing was the smallest coin worth ¼d or about one tenth of a penny). There was also a special "Salvage Drive" and 1 ton 11cwt 108lbs. was collected. However, the most successful effort was "Wings for Victory" week in June, 1943 when more than £9,000 was raised in the Parish. By 1944 Lady Cripp's "Aid to China Fund" was being supported.

A notable example of fund raising for the "Aid to Russia Fund" was by the Partridge Green Youth Club's production of "Merry March Hares" (see photo opposite). This was performed in the Partridge Green Village Hall on 27th-29th March and 1st April, 1943 and also in Cowfold. The following report was published in the "West Sussex County Times":

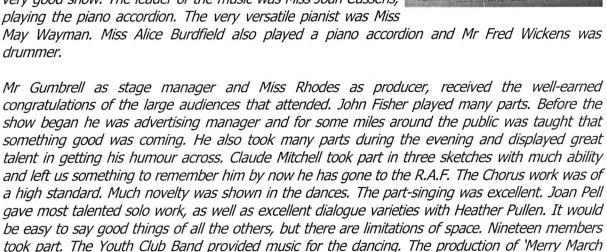

"Under the title of the 'Merry March Hares' the youth club put up a very good show. The leader of the music was Miss Joan Cussens, playing the piano accordion. The very versatile pianist was Miss May Wayman. Miss Alice Burdfield also played a piano accordion and Mr Fred Wickens was drummer.

Mr Gumbrell as stage manager and Miss Rhodes as producer, received the well-earned congratulations of the large audiences that attended. John Fisher played many parts. Before the show began he was advertising manager and for some miles around the public was taught that something good was coming. He also took many parts during the evening and displayed great talent in getting his humour across. Claude Mitchell took part in three sketches with much ability and left us something to remember him by now he has gone to the R.A.F. The Chorus work was of a high standard. Much novelty was shown in the dances. The part-singing was excellent. Joan Pell gave most talented solo work, as well as excellent dialogue varieties with Heather Pullen. It would be easy to say good things of all the others, but there are limitations of space. Nineteen members took part. The Youth Club Band provided music for the dancing. The production of 'Merry March Hares' was a great success and over £66 has been sent to Mrs Churchill's Aid to Russia Fund.

The club will welcome any new members of 14 to 21 years of age. The yearly subscription is 2s and 6d. EAK"

In December 1943 the children at Jolesfield School received a letter from a man on active service in thanks for a parcel of cigarettes sent. This is an extract:

"Dear Boys and Girls,

It would be just too bad if no one could find the time to write you a letter of thanks for the smokes you sent us. They went up in smoke in no time. We like to be remembered by the folks at home, especially when something comes of it! Rest assured we will do our best to win the war quickly so that you can eat bananas again, and come out of the pictures without tripping over in the black-out.

There are hundreds of children in the towns here. They're just like yourselves except that they speak a different language. I wish you could get to know them so that future wars could be avoided. To hear some folk at home speak you'd think they grow nothing but bayonets in the gardens here, but they don't, you know. And so I hope you'll start asking grown-ups lots of questions. We shall win the war all right, but if you don't insist on knowing the truth about everything we shall lose the peace.... It's not much good catching a bus unless you know

Below is a photograph of the cast of the Partridge Green Youth Club production of "Merry March Hares" in 1943

Back Row (left to right)

Joan Cussens, Bill Bacon, Gilbert Fairs, Fred Wickens, John Fisher, Michael Cussens, Claude Mitchell, Jean Gale, George Gumbrell

Middle (left to right)

Marjorie Rhodes, Pam Cribb, Rita Barnet, Joan Pell, May Wayman, Joyce Burdfield, Beryl Burdfield, Geoff Mitchell, Eric Priestley

Front Row (left to right)

Bill Tidey, Hilda Burdfield, Lilian Lucas, Heather Pullen, Alice Burdfield

where you're going is it? And remember for every flea you see on a foreigner's dog there may be two on yours. Let's make sure there are no holes in our own socks before we look at other people's.

Good-bye for now children and a very Happy Christmas to you. Thanks again...."

One of the most successful sources of fundraising were the regular dances held in both Partridge Green and Dial Post Village Halls. However, after D-Day in June 1944 and the departure of most of the locally based soldiers attendances dropped dramatically and they became much less frequent. Now it was prisoners of war who became the main target for raising funds and sending parcels. By 1945 special parties and receptions were being arranged for returning P.O.W.s and each was presented with a "parcel of bank notes".

Below are some memories of fundraising:

Local Girls' War Effort
By Wendy Pennifold (née Tidey, born at Fernlea)

I have recalled the time during the war when Pam Fogarty and four other girls raised money by holding a Fete and Show in the Burdfield's garden in South Street (the best place to live with fields nearby). The four other girls were Rita Carter (née Barnett), Heather Pullen (and evacuee living with the Burdfields), Olive Harrison (née Saunders) and Hilda Burdfield (the late Hilda Goldsmith); they were 12/13 years old.

I assume the money raised was for the war effort and it seemed to me that the whole village supported these events. I remember there were games and stalls at the Fete and I bought three woollen balls to hang on the hood of my dolls pram, they were really made for babies' prams. I also won a golliwog in the raffle – that would not be permitted nowadays. I think music was played for the dancing in the show, a piano I think and I remember fairies in fairylike costume and Pam being a witch (good grounding for her future drama career) and amazing acrobatics being executed. I thought it was wonderful and so Sheila Pullen and I decided to get up a show. We rehearsed in my garden in South View Cottages with Betty and Hilda Saunders but made the mistake of asking a few boys to take part – Clarence Woolven, Ron Child, Ben Sayers and my brother Keith. Sheila, a romantic, choreographed a dance but the boys objected to putting their arms around the girls' waists and when it came to acrobatics they just messed about and so this venture had to end on the second rehearsal!

To get back to the older girls' successful Fete and foray into the entertaining world – they must have spent many hours rehearsing and I suppose they had some adult help, especially with costumes. I wonder how much money they raised and if anybody can remember these events? If they had taken place at the present time the girls would most likely receive an award of sorts but during the war there would not have been such things.

It seems strange to me now but I was in awe of these 'big girls' and couldn't wait to be a Girl Guide like they were. I believe Pam was Patrol Leader of the Robins, Rita of the Red Rose and Heather and Olive were in the White Heather patrol into which I was enrolled.

Memory from Doug Pennifold

There always seemed to me to be something going on in the Village Hall to raise money for the war effort in some shape or form. There was a dance every Saturday night (organised I think by Cyril Fisher from the post office). These tended to get overrun by Canadian soldiers. These soldiers also put on a show or two and I remember "Talent Nights" when anybody and everybody got up to do a turn. One poor chap tried to sing and didn't know the words but it was great fun. The Youth Club that was formed in about 1941 also put on shows. It was I believe the Youth Club which later turned to putting on plays which formed the basis of what became the Village Dramatic Group.

What Happened Where — 1939 to 1945

By Colin Rudling

Note: the fold out map shows the location of many of the various events listed with numbers corresponding to those listed below.

1 **The Secret Shipley Bunker** (with data from Subterranea Britannica)

This underground hideout was built to house three women radio operators of the ATS. Their job was to pass on information gathered by local spies and agents operating in the area after an invasion.

The structure was virtually a Nissen Hut, on a concrete base, built underground and very cleverly camouflaged.

The entrance was via an earth-covered trapdoor and down a ladder. The first small room was made to look like an arms and explosives store, but a secret door led to the main chamber.

(Photo by Nick Catford)

This is the view on entering the hideout. Ventilation pipes are to the left of the doorway; the escape tunnel can be seen through the second doorway.

(Photos by Nick Catford)

The main living chamber, looking back towards the entrance shaft.

Picture shows the remains of electrical wiring.

(Photos by Nick Catford)

The ventilation pipes, with the opening for the escape tunnel on the right. The shelf to the left of the doorway was for a generator driven pump to give extra ventilation if required.

Above is the emergency exit. This was at the end of a tunnel sixteen feet long and three feet wide. The wooden trap door was covered with soil.

(Photo by Nick Catford)

The radio aerial for the hideout was forty feet long and was run up this nearby oak tree. A groove was cut in the bark and the aerial embedded in it. The groove is still visible today.

Gun emplacement, 50m west of Betley Bridge (no. 30 on map)

Bines brook, used by Canadians for assault course training (no. 22 on map)

126

2 French Canadian troops billeted at Clockhouse.

3 30th November 1942 at 1321, two German fighter planes attacked West Grinstead Railway Station with machine gun fire, killing a train driver, George Ansbridge. (See also page 44)

4 19th July 1940, a Spitfire made a forced landing in West Grinstead Park, having been damaged when attacking a German bomber over Partridge Green, the pilot was unhurt. The bomber is believed to have been shot down over the sea.

5 24th December 1940, at 1503, one unexploded bomb.

6 French Canadian troops were stationed at West Grinstead Park.

7 Knepp Castle was the Forward Headquarters of the First Canadian Army.

8 28th October 1940, at Lancasters Farm, one incendiary bomb, no damage.

9 21st December 1940 at 1940, three high explosive bombs, slight damage to Chucks Farm.

10 RAF Beaufighter R2120 crashed into a wood at Needs Farm on 13th February 1941.

The aircraft was flying on a night exercise when it began to vibrate violently, the pilot, Sergeant Pilot David Victor Gee, and his radar operator baled out safely. He was killed on March 21st 1941 when his Beaufighter, R2070, dived into the ground at Manor Farm Eastergate. (See also page 45)

11 26th September 1940 St. Hugh's Charterhouse hit by two high explosive bombs and one unexploded bomb. Extensive damage to buildings, a valuable library buried in rubble and another endangered. Living quarters were evacuated.

Dom Francis was in Cell K, which was destroyed, he escaped unhurt apart from his hearing, which was badly and permanently damaged. A monk in the cell next door escaped unharmed.

There was a small detachment of Canadian Signals personnel stationed at the Monastery. They were housed in accommodation sectioned off from the Monks.

The Home Guard had an observation post just below the clock tower where they kept a vigil. However the generous supper provided by the monks, of bread, cheese and a flagon of cider, was not conducive to eagle-eyed scrutiny of the night skies!

A small number of the monks served in the armed forces during the war, returning to the monastery afterwards.

As with other Germans in Britain during the War, German monks were sent to Internment Camps, along with other foreigners who could not prove they were not German.

12 29th May 1941 at 0250 St. Hugh's bombed again, one high explosive bomb; there was slight damage to the roof of the Guest House and one window broken.

13 A British Army Searchlight Unit was based at Littleworth.

14 Home of Mr Chaplin (Gunsmith). Many years after the war we learnt that he had been a member of a secret unit of the Home Guard, trained in the use of explosives, sabotage and silent killing. This unit would have fought on behind enemy lines had we been invaded. The life expectancy of this squad in action was two weeks.

26th September 1940: St Hugh's Charterhouse hit by two high explosive bombs and one unexploded bomb.

Photographs courtesy of John Winstanley

15   V1 Flying Bomb (Doodlebug) exploded on 6th July 1944 at 0345.

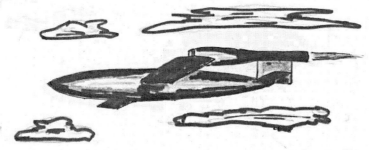

Colin Rudling

At 0345 on the 6th July 1944 a V1 Flying Bomb (Doodle Bug) crashed and exploded in a field to the west of Church Road and almost opposite St. Michael's Church, leaving a crater 4m wide and 2m deep.

*Joy Gibson, née Mitchell, in what remains of the crater formed by the V1, looking east with Church Road in the background.
(See also p131 and p18)*

The V1 had been flying on a course from southeast to northwest, so had only narrowly missed the built up area of the village. Two bungalows were badly damaged, there was slight damage to the Church and to Jolesfield House, but there were no casualties.

The worst of the blast seems to have gone to the east from the point of impact. I was sleeping at my grandmother's house in Peacock Row in the High Street; the bedroom window was open and the curtain rail and curtains were blown across the room.

Herbert Mitchell (butcher) was renting the field for grazing at the time. Luckily the twenty four cattle and a horse that were in the field were lying down in a hollow at the time, so escaping the blast and flying fragments. The animals were frightened, but none were harmed.

The field was sealed off to keep people away from the site, but Herbert Mitchell was allowed in to tend the livestock. His young daughter Joy took every opportunity to go with him and collect whatever small scraps of wreckage she could find, as these were a valuable form of currency to use in the school playground.

16   Holding area for tanks and motorised heavy guns during the build up to D Day.

17   Shermanbury Grange, headquarters of the Second Royal Canadian Signals, and later the Third Royal Canadian Signals Regiment.

18   Canadian troops were billeted at Ewhurst Manor.

19   Prisoner of war compound.

20   29th May 1941, one high explosive bomb near Lock Bridge, no damage or casualties.

21 Approximate route of a "Tank Road", constructed because the bridge over the railway was not strong enough to take the weight of heavily armoured vehicles.

22 Bines brook, used by Canadians for assault course training. (see picture on p126)

23 Rows of huts were here to accommodate troops.

24 11th Canadian Army Tank Battalion (Ontario Regiment) were based at Shermanbury Place.

25 Shermanbury Water Mill (above) Built c 1777, it was burnt down by Canadian troops 1944. There was no clear evidence as to the cause, but it was believed to have been accidental.

26 28th July 1941 at 0243, German bomber (Ju 88) crashed in flames, having been shot down by an RAF Beaufighter. (see pages 133 and 17)

27 2nd October 1942, Spitfire of 501 Squadron flown by Pilot Sergeant H. Kelly made a forced landing, having run out of fuel. The pilot was unhurt and the plane was repaired and flew again.

28 **29** Gun emplacements to defend Mock Bridge.

31 **32** Gun emplacements to defend Bines Bridge.

30 **34** Gun emplacements to defend Betley Bridge.

Joy Gibson (née Mitchell) in the crater made by the V1 Flying Bomb (Doodlebug) that landed near Church Road on July 6th 1944. The engine of the V1 became lodged half way up the tree in the background.

33 4th November 1940 at 1645, German JU 88 bomber dropped two high explosive bombs, causing only slight damage to the railway track and missing its probable target, Betley Bridge (below).

35 6th November 1940 at 2125, one high explosive bomb, no casualties, some windows broken.

36 29th October 1940 at 2210, one high explosive bomb, no damage.

37 22nd November 1943 at 2100, two high explosive bombs at Binser's Barn, Daylands Farm, no damage

38 Area used by Royal Canadian Engineers to practise the construction of Bailey Bridges, prior to the invasion of France on D Day.

39 7th December 1940 at 0030, one high explosive bomb and one incendiary bomb, no casualties, slight damage to house and farm buildings.

The Junkers 88 Crash

Colin Rudling

Luftwaffe Junkers Ju 88

At 0243 on the 28th. July 1941 a German Junkers 88 bomber that was thought to be engaged in a raid on London, was shot down by an RAF Bristol Beaufighter of 219 Squadron based at Tangmere. Crew members were Pilot Officer Hodgkinson and Sergeant Dye, who both visited the scene later in the day.

Colin Rudling

Royal Air Force Bristol Beaufighter

The incident was reported in the Southern Weekly News. These are edited extracts:

The stricken bomber burst into flames and exploded before crashing in pieces to the west of Bines Road and south of the top of Lock lane (no 26 on map).

Parts of the plane tore through the centre roof of two semi-detached cottages, blazing oil setting fire to the rafters and the beds below them. One engine hurtled through a summer house and a bedroom window, and came to rest, streaming black oil, half way through a dividing wall, and within inches of a pillow occupied up to a few minutes earlier by Rosemary, four year old daughter of Mrs Clara Hemsley, of Weald Cottage bungalow.

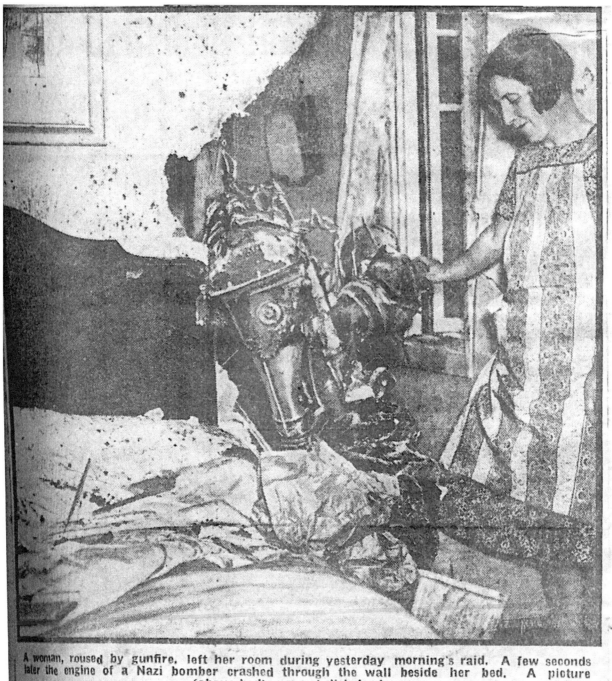

A woman, roused by gunfire, left her room during yesterday morning's raid. A few seconds later the engine of a Nazi bomber crashed through the wall beside her bed. A picture (above bed) was not dislodged

Hearing machine gunning overhead Mrs Hemsley, who had never got up before because of an air raid, acted on sudden impulse, and gathering her daughter in her arms, she shepherded 12 year old evacuee Joan Cavalier into the adjoining room.

Hardly had they got through the bedroom door when they were all thrown to the ground, and lying on the bed vacated less than two minutes earlier was part of an aircraft engine weighing several hundredweights. It had come clean through the window, and on the pillow where young Rosemary's head had been was a piece of masonry two feet square.

"I don't know what made me get up" said Mrs Hemsley. "It was a miracle, for I have never bothered about raids before, but this time something other than myself urged me to leave the room. Perhaps it was the spirit of our kind old friend Rev. Mr Johnson, watching over us. He knew me as a little girl, later I became his housekeeper, and when he retired he came to live with my husband and myself. He died a short while ago at the grand age of 98".

Mr and Mrs Smith who were also in the bungalow were not affected.

134

Flaming oil set fire to the cottages occupied by Mr and Mrs W Pennifold and their two young sons on one side and Mrs R A Laker, aged 70 and her brother in law, Mr James Laker, aged 84, and Mr B Boyce on the other. The village fire brigade was on the scene within five minutes, and quickly subdued the fires, leaving a charred and gaping hole in the roof.

The mutilated body of a German airman was found in the rafters, and removed by PC Holdstock. The remains of three other members of the crew were found scattered with the wreckage of their plane over a wide area, along with other personal effects. This was all collected up by Police Auxiliary Sergeant Herbert Mitchell and stored at his house, to be collected by MOD officials the following day.

Love token carried by a Junkers crew member and found by Mr Coultrup (see page 10)

Apart from shock, no resident of the eight cottages affected by the crash, suffered from injury, other than slight scratches.

Mr and Mrs Pennifold were awakened by the roar of the diving bomber. They saw a bright flash, and as the ceiling bulged in they sprang out of bed. Almost immediately the rafters were in flames. Mrs Laker next door had the same experience. She went to her brother in law's room and awakened Mr Boyce. Her son, Christopher Boyce, came from his house across the road and helped carry Mr Laker, who is an invalid, downstairs. By that time the roof was on fire. Mr R Russell of Pinland Farm has offered a cottage to the Pennifolds. Mrs Laker and Mr Laker will stay with her son until the cottage is habitable again, and Mrs Hemsley intends to remain in her bungalow, having made arrangements for the necessary repairs.

Piled up wreckage of the Junkers Ju 88

By the time the Southern Weekly News reporter left the scene the village's contribution towards the salvage drive was assuming imposing proportions. A pile of Junkers metal was steadily mounting as people came in with fragments.

Tributes were paid to the local Fire Brigade by those who had suffered from the raid. Under Chief Officer G Simmons, First Officer R Tidey and Second Officer W J Hemsley, they were quickly on the scene, coping with hose lengths just adequate to reach the nearest source of water at Moat Farm, 2,000 yards distant.

The local WVS members assisted with fresh clothing and by storing hastily rescued articles of attire. Cups of tea were handed round by Mr and Mrs W H Darrington, and Mrs H Green, district area organiser for the WVS, was early on the scene.

An account of the night of the crash by Geoff Merritt of Elm House, Bines Road, as told to him by his mother Mrs Audrey Merritt.

My mother, together with a neighbour, Mrs Florence Lucas, were "fire watchers", trained to deal with any small outbreaks, armed with their bucket of water and stirrup pump, items which were of no use to them on the night of the plane crash. According to my mother, most things were alight, including the trees.

My mother's Aunt Alice, my grandmother's sister, decided to visit the family in the country, to get away from Sutton and the nightly air raids on London. She duly travelled by train to Partridge Green on Sunday 27th July, looking forward to a relaxing few days in the country. Who would have thought that the very same night a plane would crash close to the house she was staying in. As soon as she could the next day she packed her bags and went back to Sutton, declaring that it had been a far worse experience than any of the air raids.

A more gruesome tale concerned our next-door neighbour, Mr William Darrington, who, awakened by the noise of the crash got up to investigate. On opening his front door he was startled when a leg complete with boot and sock fell onto the door mat. It had been propped up against the outside of the door.

My mother also told me about another neighbour, whose name I have sadly forgotten, who found a rubber life raft in her front garden. When the soldiers were clearing up she asked them to inflate it, climbed in, and sang "Red Sails in the Sunset". Talk about wartime spirit!

There was a machine gun from the crashed plane, which came to rest under a hedge. The authorities knew it was there, but it went missing. This caused a bit of a stir, word went round that there would be trouble if it was not found. It mysteriously reappeared under the hedge, and the matter was closed.

A propeller from one of the engines passed directly over our house, and landed in an orchard which is now part of Mr Peter Holt's garden. I wonder if that was when we lost our chimney pots?

My mother told me that the next day the pilot responsible for shooting down the Junkers came to survey the damage he had caused, and to apologise to everyone. He said he had tried to turn the Junkers back over the sea, but the German pilot was having none of it, so he had no alternative but to shoot it down, to avoid it reaching London.

Small fragments of metal can still be found in the field where the plane crashed, especially after the ground has been ploughed. I have a piece of bent aluminium with traces of grey paint on it that I picked up about 15 years ago. If you know where to look I expect the mark left by a burning tyre on the end of Mrs Ann Murrray's house is visible, probably faded with time, but very distinct when I was younger.

Debris from an engine from the Junkers Ju 88

An account of the crash by Doug Pennifold who also lived in Bines Road and was ten years old at the time.

The Junkers 88 exploded on landing – not bombs, but the diesel tanks, so that everything was blown to pieces. There were no plane or plane parts in the field where it hit the ground. Debris and burning oil flew everywhere; trees and hedges were alight as well as the roof of our house, from where the firemen extracted a part torso of a German, I saw it in the neighbour's garage the next morning, before going to school as usual. I think I should put in a claim for not having counselling. I had just one nightmare and then got on with enjoying our summer stay at Pinlands Farm, while the house was being repaired. I remember finding my rabbit hutch alight and put that out; then I found a stirrup pump and bucket and tried to put out a burning hedge (not at all concerned that our house was alight). Andrew Laker and I were enjoying ourselves. Then Herbert Mitchell (Special Constabulary) arrived and sent me off to spend the rest of the night with Geoff (his son), at his house, I shared a bed with Geoff, before returning to the scene soon after

Herbert Mitchell, farmer and local butcher, was the Senior Auxiliary Police Officer during the war.

daybreak. I think I might have worn Geoff's clothes to school. Imagine walking from our house to the Butchers in pyjamas.

I believe the other half of the engine fell in a field in Shermanbury or Wineham. The Junkers was being tailed by a night fighter, a Beaufighter I think, and they hoped to attack it when it got over the Channel. It turned back, however, and they had to attack for fear of losing it. We lay in bed and heard the cannon fire. The crew came up from Tangmere to see what damage had been done. They were very concerned to see a burning house and stayed on patrol in the area to safeguard us from further attack. They were on a train back to Tangmere when I went to school at Steyning.

My lasting memory is the smell of destruction, oil and perhaps the stench of bits of human body (or so I imagined) which pervaded the area for a long time. The ARP went round with sacks picking up the bits!!

There were no deaths or injuries to any civilians; a man in one of the cottages slept through the lot!

There was always a certain mystery about the Junkers crew and what it was doing, because all the name tags recovered showed the "crew" to be all quite highly ranked. The question was that if they had raided London and were heading home, why take a route over Sussex and why turn back when fuel would have been precious?

Were they doing a 'Hess'??"

Operation Sidecar — Gliders at Dial Post

By Colin Rudling

At 1140AM on the 18th of April 1944 forty-eight gliders landed in the fields between Dial Post and Hooklands Lane (see fold-out map).

This was probably the most significant military event in our area, yet very few local people seem to have been aware of it, both at the time and to this day.

The main objects of the exercise were:-

(1) To test the ability of pilots to land in a selected area.

(2) To ascertain the minimum size of fields required for satisfactory glider landings.

(3) To test the glider capacity of individual fields.

(4) To evaluate the effectiveness of the glider force, in equipment and troops, for battle after landing.

(5) To find the length of time for the airborne force to form up, with equipment, at a selected rendezvous point.

The exercise, code named "SIDECAR", was an American operation involving the 101st Airborne Division and 437 Group, part of the 53rd Carrier Wing which was based at Ramsbury Airfield near Marlborough in Wiltshire. The landing site was chosen because the countryside was very similar to that in Normandy, where the D-Day invasion was being prepared for. The glider pilots had to be able to land in small fields no longer than 350 yards that were surrounded by high hedges and large trees. The gliders used in this exercise were the British built "Horsa", and the smaller American built CG-4A "Waco".

The Royal Air Force was kept informed of the operation, but seem to have played no active part in it. The British Meteorological Office supplied weather information.

On the 15th April, three days before the landings, a team of fifty men went to the site to rehearse their ground duties. Flares were to be put on the lanes surrounding the landing area, white stripes were laid in fields, a "Eureka" homing device was to be installed and four movie cameras to be put in place. Aerial still and movie pictures were also to be taken. (see page 140)

Initially the landings were planned to take place at dawn, which is the time that the D Day landings would be, but this was later considered too hazardous and the time was changed to 1140am. The local Lands Officer was ordered to make sure all that all land owners and farmers in the landing zone were made aware of the landings, and to clear their fields of livestock.

The force consisted of eight Horsas and forty Waco gliders. They took off in four flights, fifteen minutes apart. The Horsas were each loaded with a Jeep combined with a 57mm gun, or a Howitzer gun, or with a similar weight of ammunition. Twelve of the Wacos were loaded with either a Jeep, a Howitzer, a 57mm gun or ammunition. The other twenty Wacos were loaded with sandbags to simulate a normal operational cargo.

Each glider had a pilot and co-pilot, but no troops were on board. The crews who would normally be on board to unload the cargo were waiting at the landing zone; this was a precautionary measure to minimise casualties.

The forty Waco gliders were fitted with tail parachute brakes, which were a new development to most of the pilots.

The gliders used in Operation Sidecar

The British built Airspeed Horsa glider was made completely of wood, had a wingspan of 88 feet and was 67 feet long. The load capacity was 7,750lbs.

The American built CG-4A Waco was made of fabric covered wood and had a metal frame. Smaller than the Horsa, it had a wingspan of 84 feet and was 49 feet long. Its load capacity was around 3,700 lbs.

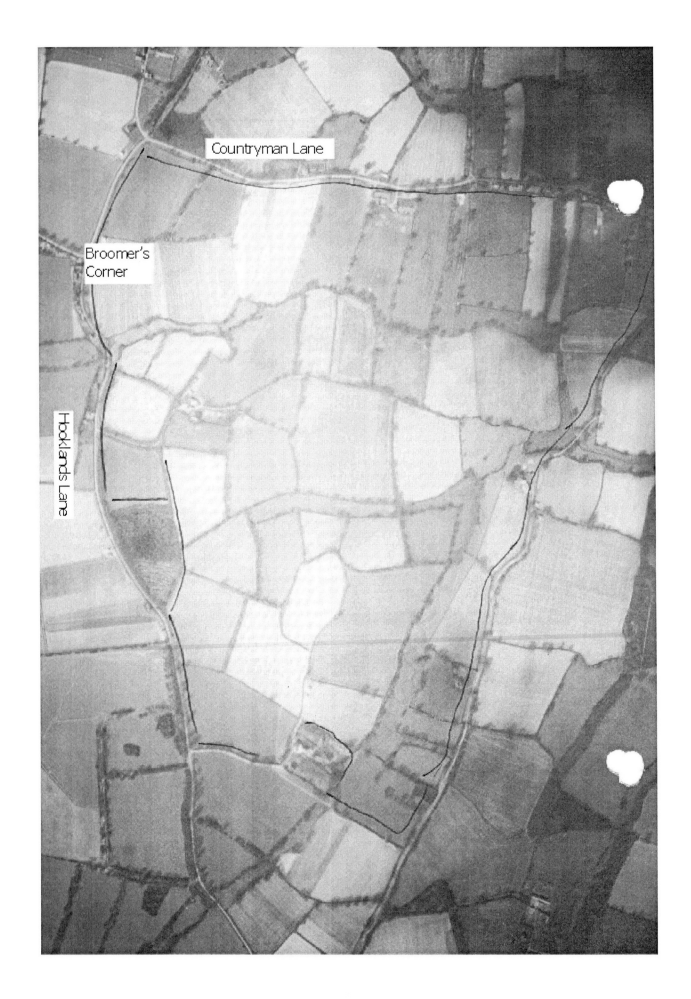

Aerial photograph taken prior to Operation Sidecar with target area marked

The force arrived over the landing zone at 1140am and at about 1000ft. It was completely landed within 5-10 minutes. Only one glider landed outside an area of 1 square mile; another five landed just outside the designated zone. Officers on the ground watching the landings reported that the pilots did a "superior job" landing their gliders in the fields, which were, if anything, smaller than the fields they would be using in France. The pilots had not seen the landing area before except on maps and photos.

Less than one hour after the last glider had landed, one glider had been retrieved by the automatic pick-up device. This was to continue with all gliders that were flyable.

Glider recoveries or "snatches" as the crews called them, were carried out as follows. One end of a nylon towrope was attached to the glider's nose. Two 12 foot poles, placed twenty feet apart, supported the other end of the 350 foot long towrope, which was formed into a loop in the centre of the two poles. The tug aircraft, usually a C47 Dakota, with a twenty foot long arresting hook hanging down from the tail flew over at about 40 feet above the ground. The hook was attached to a cable that was wound around a steel drum within the tow plane. With the Dakota flying over the glider and elevated towrope sling, the hook "snatched" the glider's towline at 110mph. The glider was airborne in about three seconds.

The location of the landed gliders is shown on page 142.

Gliders numbered 5 (Horsa), 6 (Horsa) and 19 (Waco) made crash landings. Casualties would have occurred had personnel been riding in those gliders. All the other gliders made safe landings.

The gliders were fairly well concentrated in the landing area. However no attempt was made to land the Waco gliders that contained a howitzer or gun section close to a glider carrying a jeep that would be towing it after the landing. The larger Horsa gliders had the advantage that they could carry both Jeep and howitzer. This exercise showed that the Wacos needed to land in pairs, in order to speed up the unloading process.

Landing reports for all gliders that carried military equipment

(Gliders numbered 1 to 8 were all Horsas; gliders 9 to 20 were all CG-4A Wacos)

No. 1
Nose wheel was broken and forced up through the floor of glider. Right wheel lost on landing. Glider was cocked forward and to the right. The upper left bolt bound and required ten minutes to get loose. Too much time was spent trying to pry off the split nut, rather than removing the bolt with a wrench. Load: Jeep and Howitzer.

No. 2
Left wheel lost in landing. Studs to hold troughs for unloading broke. Twisting strain caused steel plate to break off. Personnel steadied troughs for actual unloading. Load: Jeep and Howitzer.

No. 3
No difficulties encountered during unloading. Blocked road caused delay reaching the assembly area. Load: Jeep and Howitzer.

No. 4
Studs to hold unloading troughs broke while Jeep was being unloaded. Blocked road delayed reaching the assembly area. Load: Jeep and ammunition.

No. 5
Glider crash landed across road. Nose wheel broke and came up through the floor. Right wheel lost on landing. Front unloading door broken. Tail section sticking up in the air. Load removed by chopping out right side of glider. Load: Jeep and ammunition.

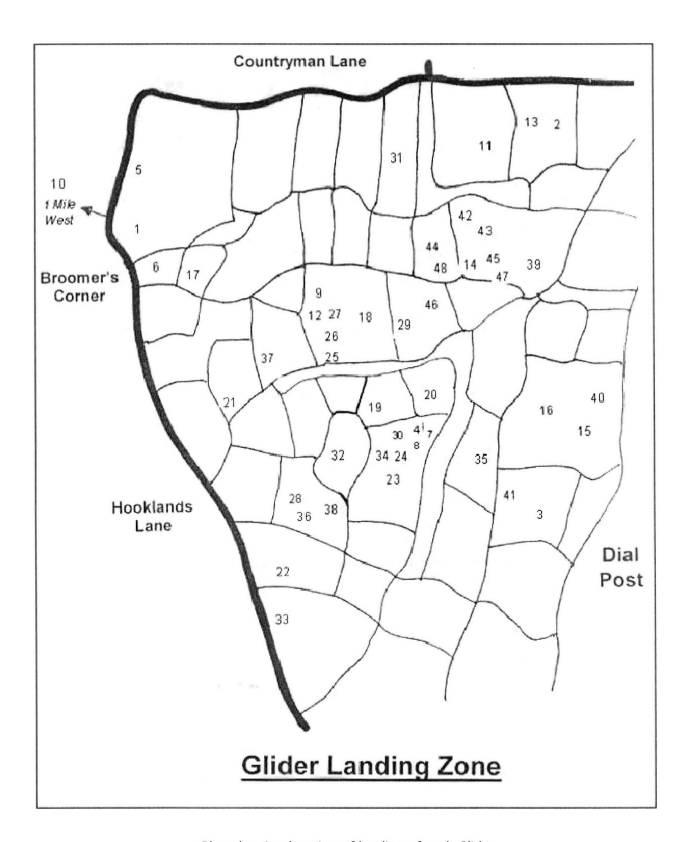

Countryman Lane

10
1 Mile
West

Broomer's
Corner

Hooklands
Lane

Dial
Post

Glider Landing Zone

Plan showing location of landing of each Glider

No. 6

Glider crash landed. Left wing hit a tree and landing gear caught in a ditch, stopping the glider suddenly. The Jeep and trailer broke loose and went through the front of the glider, ending up about ten feet away.

The Jeep had been lashed with six lashings, four to prevent forward motion, two to prevent rearward motion. Standard lashings require only four lashings on a Jeep.

The trailer had been lashed with four lashings, two forward and two rear, as prescribed.

The landing washed out the floor of the glider back to bulkhead No. 3, and the forward lashings of the trailer. Four broken chains and two broken strainers remained at the glider at the inspection. This accounts for six of the remaining eight lashings on the equipment. The sergeant in charge of the load reported that air corps officers had taken a couple of broken chains with them. One tiedown ring at frame No 15 to which the Jeep had been lashed was torn loose from the glider.

Conclusions

(1) The equipment had been properly lashed with two extra lashings on the Jeep.

(2) The excessive landing shock caused the lashings to break. Due to the number of broken lashings, it is concluded that the lashing equipment was not defective.

(3) It is recommended that no additional lashings be required on Jeeps and trailers.

No. 7

No difficulties encountered in unloading. Load: Jeep and trailer.

No. 8

Nose wheel of glider was broken and forced up through the floor behind pilot compartment. Nose section split loose from cargo compartment most of the way round. Tail of glider was up in the air. Nose wheel coming through floor prevented unloading by the front loading door. As the nose section was loose it was deemed easier to remove it completely to unload by the front unloading door.

Steps necessary to get the nose off.

(1) Cut top frame of door with a saw.

(2) Cut three metal air lines at upper right side of bulkhead.

(3) Cut all wiring.

(4) Cut control cables. All control cables are located under the floor, three on each side and two in the centre.

(5) Cut metal longerons (longerons are long spars, running fore and aft in the fuselage of the glider) at top of glider with an axe, and two cables inside each longeron.

(6) Push nose off. With the nose off and the equipment in place the glider is tail heavy. When the nose was pushed off, the front of the cargo compartment raised up and the front wheel fell off. With the nose off, the Horsa glider is about balanced at the wheels. Moving equipment forward brought the nose down to the ground. The floor level was close enough to the ground to unload the Jeep and trailer without using troughs or other aids.

This method of unloading was only practical as the nose section of the glider had been split loose in landing. It would not be practical to cut the nose section completely off.

Unloading Times for Horsa Gliders:

Glider No.	Bolts Removed	Troughs in Place	Unloading Completed	Arrival at Assembly Area	Remarks
1	17 mins	19.5 mins	20.25 mins	26.5 mins	
2	2.5 mins	13 mins	14 mins	15 mins	
3	6.75 mins	8 mins	9.25 mins	30 mins	
4	6 mins	7 mins	12.12 mins	23 mins	
5			20 mins	23 mins	Unloaded through side
6					Crash landed
7	5 mins	9 mins	11 mins	22 mins	
8			25 mins	30 mins	Unloaded through nose

Unloading Times for CG-4A Gliders:

Glider No.	Type of Load	Unloading Completed	Jeep to Weapon	Arrival at Assembly	Remarks
10	Jeep				Landed 1 mile from area. Pilot and co-pilot unloaded prior to arrival of troops.
9	Jeep	1 min	2 min	8 min	
11	Howitzer	0.5 min			Jeep from no. 9
12	Howitzer	1 min	24 min	29 min	Jeep from no. 9 (second trip)
13	Jeep	25 min	29 min	33 min	* see note below
14	Howitzer	3 min			Jeep from no. 13
15	Jeep	8 min		22 min	
16	57mm Gun	3 min			Jeep from no. 15
17	Jeep	3 min	7 min	26 min	
18	57mm Gun	5 min			
19	57mm Gun	5 min			Gun got bogged down. Never reached the area.
20	Jeep	10 min	22 min		

* Glider no. 13

Glider crash landed with nose section against a building so that it was impossible to unload through the nose. The metal frame on the right side was cut with an axe at the rear personnel door. A Jeep was used to bend the tail section out of the way so the Jeep in the glider could be removed.

This aerial photograph was taken soon after the landings, and covers about two thirds of the landing area

Initial General Conclusions

Captain James M Robinett, Field Artillery Liaison Officer, made the following assessment immediately after the landings:

(a) Equipment can be removed from crashed gliders of either type within half an hour provided the equipment itself is not damaged.

(b) Gliders can be landed in a limited area composed of small fields without an undue number of casualties and loss of equipment.

(c) Gun sections, or Jeep and trailer can be assembled from two CG4A Waco gliders without loss of time provided they are landed close to each other or the Jeep driver knows the location of the weapon or trailer. Identifying markings on the gliders to indicate a prime mover or towed load would aid assembling after landing.

(d) Glider leaders will use ingenuity in unloading gliders that have crash landed.

Two days after the exercise the following evaluation was made:

1. The value of the glider rehearsal carried out by 437 Group of IX.T.C.C. on the 18th April, was to a large extent discounted by the fact that it was not carried out until 1145AM when weather and light conditions were good.

2. The test was carried out more as a demonstration than a rehearsal, and the postponement of the landing from the dawn hour for which it was fixed was unfortunate as the weather conditions at dawn appeared satisfactory, though undoubtedly more difficult.

3. The following factors made the exercise easier than under operational conditions:-

 (a) The flight to the target was carried out in good weather conditions and wholly by daylight. It lasted for forty minutes instead of about two hours. There was no enemy opposition. Navigation was easy.

 (b) Considerably more reconnaissance of the landing area had taken place than could occur over enemy territory.

 (c) The marking of the area was exceptionally clear and lavish. Large white strips and coloured smoke were laid out all around the area, which must have been very easy to see from the air.

 (d) The landing took place in full daylight without ground opposition.

4. The results of the landings as far as the gliders are concerned were as follows:-

Gliders

Landed outside area, or in fields not assigned to them	12.5%
Bad damage	15%
Less badly damaged	43%
Undamaged	27.5%
Special glider for demonstration (?)	2%
	100%

50% of the gliders landed outside what was understood to be the fields selected for landings. 3% of the glider pilots taking part were injured, none seriously; it appeared that about 2% of the equipment in the gliders would have been badly damaged; it appeared that perhaps 5% of the troops, if carried in the gliders, might have been injured.

In short, the exercise confirmed that it is a perfectly practicable proposition to land gliders by daylight in fields of this size in peaceful conditions.

5. The following points of interest emerged from this exercise:-

(a) More than 50% of the gliders landed in fields in which they were not briefed to land.

(b) It appeared to be mainly the later gliders that landed outside the area or in the wrong field, and some of the pilots reported that this was due to their fields being already full. It appears that arable fields will not hold as many gliders as anticipated, the earth causes them to lose their undercarriages which prevents them running to the end of the field, leaving room for following gliders to land.

In my opinion the glider pilots showed great skill in landing their gliders as well as they did. The task of landing in small fields with practically no wind proved more difficult than I expected, and even the glider pilots who appeared to judge their approach accurately got into trouble. In my opinion the casualties at first light would have been far greater.

(c) Horsas. Although the approach and glide of the Horsa appeared to be much safer than that of the Waco, every Horsa over-shot rather badly or crashed. Some expert pilots said they were being flown too fast, but it was also clear that the loaded Horsa runs a long way on the ground as compared to the Waco.

Wacos. The float and glide of the Waco was so flat as to appear dangerous, but once the Waco touched down it pulled up in a very short distance. Time and time again Wacos that I thought were going to crash badly, pulled up in about twenty five yards with no serious damage.

(d) Gliders were released from between 800 and 1200 feet. Most of the pilots seemed to consider this too high, as there was congestion and risk of a collision during the glide down. I think personally this was due to the concentrated release, bad flight plan after release, and the fact that U.S. glider pilots are used to being released at a low height.

6. Ground Equipment

The collection of the ground equipment was somewhat unrealistic as insufficient gliders were carrying equipment. The point that struck me was that immediately after landing had taken place, it was impossible to tell where any particular glider had landed. I think they will have to carry a much more conspicuous means of identification.

7. Conclusion

From the point of view of "OVERLORD" the exercise does not answer the really difficult air questions to which answers were required, but it does confirm that gliders can be landed without undue casualties in daylight in areas of this nature, provided they can be towed there free from serious enemy opposition and provided there is plenty of time to collect equipment after landing.

Air Vice-Marshal H.E.P. Wigglesworth, Royal Air Force Senior Staff Officer, having read a report of the exercise, commented "All very well, but oh the losses or damage".

On the 14th May 1944, almost a month after the landings, the local Lands Officer wrote to Allied

Headquarters complaining that difficulties were being experienced in connection with the settlement of outstanding claims for damage caused by the exercise.

Various damaged gliders had not been removed, and apart from the question of further damage which may arise if and when the gliders were removed, some of them were in growing crops and therefore the longer their removal was postponed the more damage ultimately would be caused. In addition broken gates and damaged fences could not be repaired until all the damaged gliders had been removed, with the result that certain fields could not be used for cattle.

The Lands Officer requested that if the remaining wrecked gliders were not going to be removed in the near future, that permission be given to burn or otherwise dispose of them on site.

Footnote

Over 200 gliders took to the skies on the night of June 5th 1944, at the start of operation Overlord. The first wave carried Allied Paratroops whose mission it was to secure key objectives and prepare a secure landing ground for the next wave of gliders carrying Jeeps, Howitzers, anti-tank guns and ammunition.

Fighting was intense and casualties were heavy, but the main objective, to prevent the Germans reinforcing their troops resisting the D Day landings on June 6th was largely achieved, saving many lives.

Appendix 1

Partridge Green Wartime Telephone Numbers

John Fisher manned the telephone exchange in Partridge Green in the 1930s and for most of the war. In those days every call, including local ones, had to go through the manual exchange. Contact with the exchange was made by lifting the receiver – there were no dial phones then. Local calls were connected at the local exchange, but distance calls were routed through junctions at Henfield, Horsham or Brighton before being passed on further – a process that could take some time, especially if the exchanges were busy. Before the war an incoming night call would sound a bell outside John's father's bedroom, but very few nights were broken. The war changed all that, as traffic increased and all calls had to be answered within 20 seconds – a test call came every night at any hour. The exchange had to be manned 24 hours and John slept on a camp bed next to it.

All the details below were kindly provided by John Fisher and are the only records known to exist for this period.

The numbers with names and addresses that are missing were all active lines, but no other details are available.

1	Public Telephone Kiosk outside Post Office, High Street, PG
2	Jesse Tidey, Coal Merchants, The Gables, Church Road, PG
3	Tidey's Mill, Millers & Corn Merchants, High Street, PG
4	Captain Bell, Medway House, Jolesfield
5	
6	Colonel A C Watson, Wymarks, Shermanbury
7	W D Searles, Coal Merchants, Eastern Villa, Blanches Road, PG
8	Forest Stores, High Street, PG (now Co-op)
9	E & H Mitchell, Family Butchers, High Street, PG
10	Mrs Marchant, Trueflite Kennels, Old Mill House, Mill Lane, PG
11	Mrs DeVere Allen, Oatlands, Shermanbury
12	Mr F J Ferdinand, Chalfield, Shermanbury
13	
14	Mr W Craig, Kingsbarn Farm, Ashurst
15	Worsfold's Garage, Church Road, PG
16	Mr G Norrish, Red Roofs, Blanches Lane, PG
17	Mrs Blackburne, Gratwicks, Ashurst
18	Gladwin, Keepers Mead, PG
19	The Fountain Inn Public House, Ashurst. (Albert Weaver)
20	Mr Preece, Little Chancton, Blanches Lane, PG
21	Mr George Simmons, 2 New Cottages, High Street, PG
22	Miss E B Poyser, Blanches, Blanches Lane, PG
23	Mr L J Nichols, Talloaks, Wineham
24	Bishop Wood, The Rectory, West Grinstead
25	Mrs C A & Dr Tillman, Glebe Cottage, West Grinstead
26	Mrs Muriel Langton, Copyhold, Lock Lane, PG
27	Miss C Innes, Morleys, Shermanbury
28	Mr & Mrs Scatliff, Springlands, Shermanbury
29	Mr M Linward, Veranda Cottage, Blanches Lane, PG
30	Mrs E Porter, Sixberries, Ashurst
31	L R Peace, Pound Place, Mill Lane, Jolesfield
32	
33	D H Ford, Ewhurst Farm, Shermanbury
34	W Dumbrell, Wellings, Ashurst

35	Mr Griffiths, Merrions Farm, Bines Road, Ashurst
36	Miss Fields, Homelands Farm, Bines Road, PG
37	Mr Morgan & Miss Gossett, Lloyts Croft, Lock Lane, PG
38	Mr J C Garratt, Seven Oaks, Shermanbury
39	Partridge Green Post Office, High Street, PG
40	G R Ellis, Five Acres, Blanches Lane, Littleworth
41	Mrs J Sturgeon, Wilchester, Shermanbury
42	
43	
44	Mr Stroud, The Haven, Shermanbury
45	Mrs H Brown, Minster House, Blanches Lane, Littleworth
46	Mrs J Baines, Gables Guest House, Dial Post
47	Mr & Mrs Sidebottom, Jolesfield House, Jolesfield
48	Mr G Leach, Spring House, High Street, PG
49	Mr H C Lepard, Starkers Farm, Ashurst
50	The Green Man Public House, (C Lloyd), Jolesfield
51	B Jay, Pound House, Needs Hill, Jolesfield
52	Mr Hextall, Ford Farm, Ashurst
53	The School House, Jolesfield School, Jolesfield
54	Public Telephone Kiosk, (opp. Jack's Garage), Shermanbury
55	National Fire Service, (behind The Station Hotel), Church Road, PG
56	Mrs Dumbrell, Ashurst Stores, Ashurst
57	
58	Mr Copithorne, Godsmark, Ashurst
59	
60	Mr Kidd, Old Priors, PG
61	Mr Thomas, Oaklands Farm, Wineham
62	Mr Kenward, Moat Farm, Bines Road, PG
63	Public Telephone Kiosk at Dial Post
64	Andrew Harvey's Farm Office, (George Jesse), Old Lock, PG
65	St Thomas Moore's School, West Grinstead
66	Mr Ron Russell, Bines Farm, Bines Road, PG
67	The Crown Inn Public House, Dial Post
68	Guy Chantrey, Oatlands Farm, Shermanbury
69	P C Holdstock, (Charlie), Police House, High Street, PG
70	Blaker Welding, Welding Engineers, Dial Post
71	West Grinstead Post Office, (at Burrell Arms), West Grinstead
72	Miss Phylis Gates, Merryfields (Dairy Herd), Church Road, PG
73	Rev H C Fincham, Priests House, Catholic Church, West Grinstead
74	Mr & Mrs Wiggins, Lane Cottage, Ashurst
75	Mrs Cloake, The Ivy Stores, High Street, PG
76	Mr James Ellis, Ewhurst Manor, Shermanbury
77	Mrs Butler, 18 Woodside Close, Shermanbury
78	Mr Ashford Duke, Sweethill Farm, Ashurst
79	J Mullett, Woodside, Shermanbury
80	Lord Buckmaster, Furzefield House, Wineham
81	Burrell, Floodgates, West Grinstead
82	Goacher's Stores, South Street, PG
83	William Robinson, Woodmans Farm, Dial Post
84	Miss M A Richmond, Sweetmans, Ashurst
85	Major F C Crittall, Wymering, Shermanbury
86	Mr E W Merrit, The Andes, High Street, PG
87	E G Chamings, Rookcross Farm, West Grinstead
88	Mrs Cussens, Fern Hill, Blanches Lane, PG
89	Mrs R M Dale, Westward, Brighton Road, Shermanbury

90   Mr McDonald, Starkers Farm, Ashurst
91   The Station Hotel, Church Road, PG
92   Public Telephone Kiosk, (Opp. The Fountain Inn), Ashurst
93   Miss Barnes & Miss Gibbons, Hill View, Church Road, PG
94   Mrs H Barnet, Wayside, Church Hill, PG
95   Millitary Forces at Shermanbury Grange, Shermanbury
96   Mrs Barff, Mockbridge Cottage, Shermanbury
97   Mr Hall, Glenifer, Shermanbury
98   Mr Grover, Dial Post Filling Station, Dial Post
99   Ltn. Col. O'Hea, The Capite, Dial Post
100   Mr Preece, Little Chancton, Blanches Lane, PG
101   Mr R G Danby, Toll Cottage, Brighton Road, Shermanbury
102   Mr McCrindle, Pooks Farm, Wineham
103   The Hon. Mary Hawke, Oakfield, Blanches Lane, PG
104
105   Wilton, Silver Birches, Hangar Wood, Shermanbury
106   Jack Eaton (Butcher), Mill View, Ashurst
107   Mr Beck, Needs Farm, Needs Hill, Jolesfield
108   Public Telephone Kiosk, Outside Windmill Inn, Littleworth
109   Lock Estate Workshop, (A Harvey – H Noakes), Lock, PG
110   Mr Jack Hemsley, Ventura, Church Road, PG
111   G E Owen, Eastcote, Jolesfield
112   Mr Charlton, Maryland Farm, Shermanbury
113   Nurse's Bungalow, Jolesfield
114   Miss Wright, Cloran Kennels, Brighthams, Bines Road, PG
115   William Jeffery, The Cottage, Blanches, PG
116   Mr Hornby, Wayside, Hangar Wood, Shermanbury
117   Mr & Mrs Blunden, Sunnycote, Shermanbury
118   The Burrell Arms Public House, (Moulden W), West Grinstead
119   Mr & Mrs Perfect, Guest House, Bines Road, Ashurst
120   Hopkinson, Binesfield, Bines Road, Ashurst
121   C E Newbury, Oaklea, Shermanbury
122   Miss Davies & Miss Bayley, Westlands, High Street, PG
123   Mr & Mrs Plowden, Westwinds, Church Road, PG
124   G Redman, Rookland Farm, West Grinstead
125   Dial Post Stores, Dial Post
126   Mrs Blanco-White, Greenacres, Shermanbury
127   Doctor Dickens, St Michael's Lodge, Church Road, PG
128   Mr A Harvey & Mrs Ethel Harvey, Lock House, Lock, PG
129   Mr Gladwin, Keepers Mead, Nr Monastry Wood, PG
130   Dial Post Filling Station, Dial Post
131   Miss Crittall, Hedgeways, Mill Lane, Jolesfield
132   Mansbridge Shop, (Miss Cogar L R A M) High Street, PG
133
134
135
136   Partridge Green Railway Station
137   Mr B E Chaplin, Greentree Cottage, Monastery Wood, Shermanbury
138   Mrs DuCann, Dean Cottage, High Street, PG
139   Rev G Mackenzie, The Rectory, West Grinstead
140   Mr Wonfor, Mayfield, Church Road, PG
141   Major R Hall, Glebe House, West Grinstead
142   George R Tatham, Glebe Farm, Glebe Estate, West Grinstead
143   Mrs Belman, Oak Tree Cottage, PG
144   W Dumbrell, Wellings, Ashurst

145 E Corfield, Jesmondene, Shermanbury
146 G J Kingsbury, Seven Oaks Lodge, Shermanbury
147 Mrs Blakelock, Freezers, Jolesfield
148 Mr Duncanson, Eatons Farm, Ashurst
149 Mr G J Gains, Perrylands Farm, Dial Post
150
151 Mr Heywood, Martinsland, Bines Common, Ashurst
152 Burdfield Bros. (builders), PG
153 F C Hannah, Sopers Farm, Ashurst
154
155
156 Mrs E Mitchell, Wilton Villa, High Street, PG
157 Macadam, Riverside, Shermanbury
158 Miss M Barnes, The Bushes, Blanches Lane, PG
159 Miss Ewington, Esk How, Shermanbury
160 A R Miller, Platts Green, Dial Post
161 Miss M Reith, Old Coach House Café, West Grinstead
162 M Smith, Orchard Villa, High Street, PG
163 Major Collis, Queens Gate, Shermanbury
164 H J Tidey, The Mill, High Street, PG
165
166 Knepp Castle Estate, Floodgates, West Grinstead
167
168 C L A Smith, East Lodge, Wineham
169 Mr Kirby, Sunny View, Church Road, PG
170 H F Corble, East Lodge, Wineham
171 West Sussex County Council, Shermanbury Grange, Shermanbury
172
173 P Nichols, Park View, Shermanbury
174
175 Dalkeith Poultry Farm, PG
176 Mrs Marshall, St John's Cottage, Mill Lane, Jolesfield
177 Eder Trading Farm, Grinders Lane, Dial Post
178
179
180
181
182 Mr H P Edwards, New Barn Farm, Dial Post
183
184 Wood, The Bulrushes, Mill Lane, Jolesfield
185 Luckin, Swallows Nest Farm, Dial Post
186 Mr Clark, Hazeldene, Shermanbury
187
188
189 Mr C E Bryant, Brookwood Farm, Ashurst
190
191
192
193
194
195 Mr & Mrs Barnet, Wayside, PG
196 Miss Coleman, Haynes, Blanches Lane, PG

Many of these lines that are detailed had been connected well before the outbreak of war. A few of the last higher numbers were after 1945.

The first stage of going automatic took place in a new building in 1948/9, behind a house in the High Street called 'Leeacre'. This meant that all the existing lines had to have three numbers. Thus 1-9 were prefixed with 20, 10-99 prefixed with just 2 and 100-175 prefixed with just 3. For example: 9, E H Mitchell (Butchers), became 209. 50, The Green Man Public House, became 250. 139, The Rectory West Grinstead, became 339.

The second stage, due to the demand for more lines, required a much larger building which was built at Finches Close and was fully operational in 1969. This meant that all Partridge Green numbers had to have six figures and were given the Partridge Green codes of 710 and 711 to precede the existing three numbers. This number was then preceded by the Horsham National Code Number of 0403 (now 01403) when calling from outside the Horsham area.

The small number of local telephones clearly meant that communication was much more difficult in case of emergency. Of course the telegram was then still much in use.

John Fisher with family and friends prior to the War

Back row left to right: John Fisher, his sister Rona,
Kathleen Burdfield, Mr Cyril Fisher
Front row: Joyce Burdfield, Kathleen Newman

Appendix 2

Acknowledgments

Extensive use has been made of Parish Magazine extracts, which came from the West Sussex Record Office reference Par95/7/7 deposited by West Grinstead parish churchwardens, and the Deanery Parish Magazines for Storrington II 1884 -1966 reference Par21/7/18.

Special thanks are due to the Record Office for their help and to Graham and Julie Beck for their hours of painstaking research there.

We have also made extensive use of the West Grinstead (Partridge Green and Dial Post) Newsletter. At various times articles have been printed by local people on their memories of wartime and these have been very helpful, so we give thanks to all such contributors. We are also grateful for the use of material including photographs collected for the 'Down Memory Lane' exhibitions organised by Thelma Brown to raise funds for St Catherine's Hospice.

Where we have included extracts these have been attributed to the authors in the text.

We would also like to thank the following for their help:

Doug Baker	Fred & Doris Monnery
Alan Barwick	National Archives at Kew
Janet Bryon	Brian & Daphne Norton
Sandra Budd	Jean Parker
Sir Charles Burrell	Partridge Green Methodist Church
Dr Andrew Campbell	Doug & Wendy Pennifold
Ron Child	Royal Archives Windsor Castle
Roy Coultrup	Sid & Jeanne Savage
Ken & Pam Edmonds	St Hugh's Charterhouse
John & Jean Fisher	Marcus Staples
Roy Gasson	Susannah Staples & David Tutton
Joy Gibson	Subterranea Britannica
John Hawkins	Judy Thomas
Henfield Museum	Betty Turner
Di Holman	Richard Verrall
Horsham Library	Kay Wagner
Horsham Museum	West Sussex County Times
Dennis Jenkins	West Sussex Records Office
John Jones	Barbara West
Jeremy Knight	Cliff White
Les MacDonald	John Winstanley
Geoff Merritt	Steve Wright

Appendix 3

Authors

Dorothy Banks

Dorothy, 55, is an incomer. Brought up in East Africa and Borneo, she came to Partridge Green from London, with her husband and two daughters, in 1992. Interest in local history began when she researched and mounted an exhibition to mark the centenary of the local parish council.

Colin Rudling

Colin grew up in Shermanbury, went to school at Cowfold then Collyer's. For forty years he worked for the Meteorological Office, mainly on airfields, RAF and civil, in England and overseas. In 1966 he moved with his family to Partridge Green. His interests include music, the countryside, local and family history.

Julie Beck

Julie and husband Graham farm 400+ acres in the parish of West Grinstead and produce Sussex and Limousin cattle in a non-intensive environment. The Becks have been farming in the parish for more than 80 years. Julie's interests in between cows being naughty include local history, bellringing and eating chocolate.

Derek Saunders

Derek has lived nearly all his life in Partridge Green, Cowfold and Dial Post. He served an apprenticeship with Seeboard, then studied Electronic Engineering with the Open University and served on National and European committees within the Electronic Signalling and Safety Industries. Now retired he is involved in badminton coaching and many aspects of village life with a special interest in local history.

Norman Berry (Editor)

Norman spent his early childhood in wartime Edmonton, North London and came to Partridge Green in 1968. He became interested in local history after taking it as a "fun subject" at school. He started in this because it involved wandering around the locality legally during school time.

Barbara Berry

Barbara also spent her childhood in Edmonton during the war years. She met Norman at Latymer's School and married in 1959. They had three children all educated at Jolesfield and Steyning Schools. She is a member of the Methodist Church and has lived for 40 happy years in Partridge Green.

Reginald Staples

Reg Staples was born in Dorset in 1909. In 1921 he moved to Sussex with his parents and lived at Joles Farm, Partridge Green until he died in 1991. As a farmer he had a reserved occupation and therefore joined the Home Guard in the War, becoming the First Aider. Reg was a local preacher at Partridge Green Methodist Church and was the Church Organist for 67 years from the age of 13.

Cecil Longhurst

Cecil lived his whole life in the parish of West Grinstead. He worked as a carpenter on the West Grinstead Estate and was tower captain of the bellringers. His memoirs were collected for his 90th birthday celebrations.

Doug Pennifold

Doug was born in Partridge Green and lived there throughout the war years. Being 9 years old at the outbreak of war he was at an age to be aware of many of the incidents and activities in the village and of their impact on people's lives. He still has a clear memory of village life during the war years.

Claire Walton and Peggy Bennett
by Andrew Campbell

My mother Margaret Campbell, widely known as Peggy, and her sister Claire were both born at South Lodge, Park Lane, West Grinstead, where they lived before moving up the lane to Fullers Bungalow when their father died. They shared a birthday, January 8th, but were separated by three years, Margaret being born in 1921 and Claire in 1924. As small girls they attended the Convent School at West Grinstead before both entering Horsham High School when they reached the age of 11. They travelled to school from West Grinstead Station in the company of school chums, some of whom were to remain close friends.

World War 2 had a serious effect on their lives and careers, Margaret spending much of the war nursing in London and Claire working at H.J.Burt & Co at the market office in Steyning. After the war, Margaret, now married, returned to West Grinstead parish where she immersed herself in local affairs. Through her work for the church, the WG and DP VPA, the WI and the Parish Council she developed a good grasp of local affairs and knew many people.

Claire by contrast, moved away at the end of the war and made her married home first in Wembley and then in Marlow.

The memoirs of Reg Staples, Cecil Longhurst, Doug Pennifold, Claire Walton and Peggy Bennett have been used extensively in this book - Ed.